FALLING INTO FLIGHT

Falling into Flight

A Memoir of
Life and Dance

Kaija Pepper

EDITIONS

Cover design by Doowah Design.
Photo of Kaija Pepper by Stephen Lemay.

This book was printed on Ancient Forest Friendly paper.
Printed and bound in Canada by Hignell Book Printing Inc.

We acknowledge the support of the Canada Council for the Arts and the Manitoba Arts Council for our publishing program.

Library and Archives Canada Cataloguing in Publication

Title: Falling into flight : a memoir of life and dance / Kaija Pepper.
Names: Pepper, Kaija, author.
Identifiers: Canadiana (print) 20200320602 | Canadiana (ebook) 2020032067X | ISBN 9781773240831
  (softcover) | ISBN 9781773240848 (HTML)
Subjects: LCSH: Pepper, Kaija. | LCSH: Dancers—Canada—Biography. | LCSH: Dance critics—Canada—
  Biography. | LCSH: Children of immigrants—Canada—Biography. | LCSH: Psychotherapy patients—
  Canada—Biography. | LCGFT: Autobiographies.
Classification: LCC GV1785.P46 A3 2020 | DDC 792.8092—dc23

Signature Editions
P.O. Box 206, RPO Corydon, Winnipeg, Manitoba, R3M 3S7
www.signature-editions.com

Speech is a beautiful tomfoolery:
with it man dances over all things.

Friedrich Nietzsche, from *Thus Spake Zarathustra*

The Mind Is a Muscle

Title of a choreographic work by Yvonne Rainer

Contents

I

The End of the Family Dance

MY FATHER STANDS BESIDE ME, LOOKING EXACTLY LIKE HE did the afternoon we went for a ride in his Lafarge Cement truck when I was five and he was a strong, handsome thirty-seven-year-old. I am ageless, or rather, every age: not five or sixteen or thirty-one or fifty, but carrying a whole lifetime within. It's a T.S. Eliot moment, probably inspired by dipping into *Four Quartets* nightly since Dad died. The poem's play of time on the page is comforting, not because it carries reassuring truths, but because Eliot's desire for order and sense quivers and quakes hopefully between the lines, in the words strung one after another, leading me into the dance he creates through precise, dynamic rhythm. Because I love dancing, I fall into step, and the poem moves me.

In my dream, which follows months of pondering a few pages or a few lines at bedtime — my good luck charm before sleep — in my dream I see Dad precisely, but because I'm inside myself, my own image is vague. I am definitely not a little girl anymore, but, like a child, feel reassured by his presence, though all we do is stand side by side. Nothing happens, or is going to happen, except the wonderful standing together.

I wake up glowing, filled with the sun, which floods my room with a heavenly white light. Or am I still dreaming? It takes several minutes until I'm fully back in the real world, reluctant to leave the other place behind.

WHEN DAD WAS DYING OF CANCER, I HAPPENED TO CATCH *The Shootist*, a 1976 western, on late-night TV. In it, John Wayne gives a gripping performance as J.B. Books, a gruff old gunfighter dying from cancer. I found out later the Hollywood star himself had cancer at the time he made the film, which turned out to be his last. Watching it, I couldn't stop thinking of my dad who, like John Wayne, was a tall slow-spoken man. Dad had the same stoic acceptance of his fate as J.B. Books, but instead of going out in a blaze of glory during a gunfight in a fancy saloon — dying in the blink of an eye, in one brave conscious act — my father suffered a painful lingering fade-out.

Even once his prostate cancer had metastasized to the bone and the pain in his right leg was so bad he couldn't press the gas pedal without wincing, Dad insisted on driving over to babysit on his usual Wednesday night. He enjoyed watching TV with his granddaughter, sharing the bag of potato chips he always brought, and didn't want me to miss my evening course at university. Soon, though, I was the one doing the driving, ferrying him home from radiation treatments, his leg stretched painfully out from his unfamiliar position in the passenger seat. Somehow the worst thing for both of us wasn't the radiation, but his not being behind the wheel.

Dad had never missed a day at work driving his truck around town; by the time he retired, he had a collection of badges awarded annually for being accident-free tossed in a drawer. He took me for a ride when I was in grade three. I remember gazing out the kitchen window, kneeling on one of the new blue vinyl swivel chairs, making surreptitious moves right and left — tiny so Mom wouldn't notice and tell me to stop playing on the new furniture — and spotting a cement truck lumbering up the street toward our East Vancouver corner lot. It rumbled to a stop next to our house, the noise of the barrel turning round so loud Mom came to peek out the window. "It's Andy!" she exclaimed, and I tore out the door and down the back steps.

"I finished a job a few blocks over," Dad said as he climbed from the cab. He told Mom he was on his way to Lulu Island to park his truck at the plant, then asked if I wanted a ride first. Of course I did, and he swung me up into the passenger seat. Making our way around the block, cement mixer grinding, I gazed down like a queen at the kids we passed playing on the street.

On weekends, he had happily chauffeured Mom, content to sit in his car out on the street listening to a ballgame while she bargain-hunted at the department stores. He refused to feed the meter. If anyone tried to give him a ticket, he'd say, "I'm waiting for the wife," as if that bestowed immunity. It worked; he was never ticketed.

"Oy, I'm exhausted," Mom would groan when they were back home and she was preparing dinner. "You've done nothing but sit all day!" she'd say to Dad, who might be getting himself a cold beer.

As soon as I turned sixteen, Dad taught me to drive in his big blue Parisienne. I peered over the wheel as we progressed slowly around the neighbourhood, Dad looking cramped beside me. It was partly the way he hunched forward, watching my every move like a hawk. "Easy," he warned each time I hit the brakes too hard. When another car approached, he looked sharply over to make sure I took full notice. Once he felt I was ready to face more traffic, we headed to Kingsway. "Give 'er some gas," he instructed.

I never mastered parallel parking, paying more attention to my father than to the manoeuvre itself. If I turned the steering wheel too cautiously, he'd shout, "More, more"; if I pressed on the gas too hard, he'd brace himself. When we went for my test, I still couldn't manage the quick sure moves needed to back in smoothly.

"Can you go easy on her?" Dad asked the examiner quietly, bending down and over so their faces were close together across the counter. "We're heading out to Ontario and I need help with the driving. The prairies will be a good place to get some practice in."

I passed, suspecting my driver's licence was a favour to Dad.

On flat prairie roads, my driving philosophy was established: point the car straight ahead, show no fear and hope for the best. I consistently drove too fast, beyond my abilities, but didn't want to push my foot on the brakes any more than I figured Dad would. "That's enough for today," he'd finally say. I would return with relief to join my siblings in the back seat, he'd reclaim his spot at the wheel and Mom resettled in her place beside him in the front.

THE MORNING MOM PHONED TO SAY SHE WAS WAITING FOR an ambulance to take Dad to the hospital, my first thought was confusion over why he wasn't going to drive himself. "Andy has terrible diarrhoea," she cried, and my second thought was that Dad wouldn't like her sharing news about the state of his bowels. "He insisted on taking a shower before we called the ambulance, but he hardly had the strength to get out of bed. It took so long, I've been waiting and waiting!"

"I'll meet you there," I said, and threw on some clothes, heart already pounding, thumping harder and faster as I ran the few blocks from my condo to Vancouver General Hospital's emergency entrance. An ambulance arrived, lights flashing, but he wasn't in it, sending my heart into an impossible fury. That one organ had become the only life force within me, the only one that mattered. Two more ambulances drove up; then, at last, his. Paramedics carried my father out on a stretcher, tightly wrapped in blankets, only his pale face visible, not looking like John Wayne at all.

Dad's emergency ward cot was so short that if he shifted down even a little, his feet dangled over the edge. He had a blood transfusion, which helped for a day or two. It took a week until a bed was available in the acute care ward, where doctors played about with his regimen of drugs. Increasing amounts of morphine caused constipation, the details of which I learned from nurses, not from him. At a family meeting with medical and social work staff that Dad did not attend, Mom, my three siblings and I sat miserable and long-faced, exactly the kind of attitude he would never tolerate. A social worker said it was time to find a bed in palliative care.

When we were gathered in his room afterward, Dad announced he wanted me to have the car, and said we should take care of the paperwork quickly. The instructions made sense — Mom didn't drive and my siblings already had cars — but came as a shock. It wasn't just that he usually did things fair and square — the beige Toyota Corolla should have been sold, the money divided equally among us four kids — but he'd only had it a couple of years, hardly enough time to enjoy the air conditioning on which my parents had finally splurged. We all wanted Dad behind the wheel!

On what would be my father's last evening, the air was warm and still when I arrived for my turn to sit with him in his room in the palliative care ward. Dad lay on his back, unconscious, barely breathing, the intake coming after a long period when nothing happened and it seemed his lungs would never fill again. Then — one more breath — followed by that no-man's land of breath and no-breath. My own breathing started coming too fast and hard, and I heard myself crying, so I stepped out to the visitors' area, not wanting Dad to hear.

A moment later, the nurse came running. "He's going," she said.

It was only another moment or two until I was back, but the distance between life and death is less than that, a distance too infinitesimal to count: when I threw myself onto his pale inert body, he was gone. The air around us crackled — it felt charged, vibrant, filled with his spirit, as if Dad was in the molecules of air. I told him I was glad the pain was over and that it was all right, he had to go.

FOLLOWING MY RUSSIAN MOTHER'S ORTHODOX WISHES, MY shy Finnish father was displayed in an open coffin at the funeral home. Except where the undertaker had added rouge and lipstick, his face was bloodless, colourless, and he looked shorter, shrunken, like the stuffing was knocked out of him. The service was nondenominational; Dad's roots were Lutheran, but he'd never spoken much about religion, aside from sparring with Jehovah's Witnesses who knocked at our front door.

My contribution to the gathering was a few lines from Eliot's *Four Quartets* about the complicated moments of old men's lives, and how the end is also a beginning. Dad would probably have smiled agreeably over my tearful recitation, though he was a Wordsworth man himself.

The immediate family travelled together to the cemetery in a limousine, leading the cortège, all of us sober in black, elbows and knees bumping, jammed in closer to each other than we had been for decades: my daughter and me; my siblings and their assorted partners and children; and Mom. My brothers directed the driver to take a small diversion past our Clarendon Street home, sold not long before when our parents downsized to a condo. As we drove by the sundeck Dad had built, where Mom would lie in her bathing suit soaking up the sun, I imagined him sitting there in the shade of the umbrella, wondering what the heck was going on as the hearse, the limousine and the long line of cars passed.

At the side of the grave, family and friends of Dad's crowded round as the coffin was lowered into a hole in the ground. Suddenly, in one ferocious, reality-shifting jump cut, the whole thing was happening at a distance, as if shot from a very high angle like a scene in a film, and it wasn't me trying to control my sobs but an actress playing a grieving daughter. I looked down on Mom standing quiet and shaky next to the grave, shrunken since her stroke, and was sure Dad would soon be standing next to her.

Two men from the funeral home started shovelling dirt onto the coffin, and again the view shifted, crashing into a series of close gritty details: the men, their shovels, the rain of earth into the grave. Everything was terribly real and the impossibility of a rewrite sank in. The high-angle shot returned and I watched the actress playing me throw a rose onto Dad's coffin, a sentimental gesture I'd seen in movies. Then more close-ups, this time of her face, tears streaming down, and still the camera zoomed in, closer and closer until it felt like I was inside her body. My eyes filled with tears, making it hard to see; my nose filled with a suffocating damp, making it hard to breathe.

~

WHILE DAD WAS IN PALLIATIVE CARE, MOM HAD INSISTED ON VIS-iting him every day at noon. The task of driving her fell to me: not only was I a freelance arts writer with less rigid working hours than my siblings, but Dad's car was parked in the garage at my condo. I soon realized her visits were timed for lunch. Dad didn't mind when she devoured his mashed potatoes and Jell-O, no longer interested in food himself, but it disturbed me: his last meals, and there she was scarfing them down.

When I said we'd have to go in the evenings instead because being a freelance writer didn't mean I had no responsibilities, Mom took public transit, falling on the street outside the hospital on the way back to the bus stop. A stranger rescued my mother, helping her up and driving her home. She hadn't been hurt, recounting the incident as if it was merely a nuisance and thank goodness that kind man had happened by. But I couldn't bear the thought of my mother's brittle bones and thin, easily bruised skin crashing onto the pavement again, and the next day our lunch hour visits resumed.

Later, with her diagnosis of oesophageal cancer, there was an explanation for the greedy behaviour: she had trouble swallowing, which meant she could get only the softest food down, and was slowly starving.

Once Dad was gone, Mom became so frail she couldn't get out on her own even with a walker, even just a few blocks to the hair salon, which had become a dangerous journey crossing streets filled with potholes and impatient cars. A hairdresser who visited to give a home perm covered my mother's head with a cap of tightly pinned curls. After the perm was set, when I came to help brush her hair out, Mom asked anxiously how it looked.

"Fine, it'll be easy to look after," I replied, knowing if our positions were reversed she'd have been more outspoken. "Oy," she might have sighed deeply, "it's too curly."

My mother's clothes had become big and baggy on her shrinking frame, and she was desperate to go shopping for new ones across the street at the mall. She'd called the week before around midnight, having stumbled on her way to the bathroom, toppling to the floor, too weak to get back up — I'd had to drive over and rescue her — and now she wanted to shop! "I can go on my own," she said, but of course I took her, parking as close to the entrance as possible. She only had to walk a few feet to the Bay, but the ladies' fashion department spread out in an exhausting array. In search of the perfect sweater — the right cut, the right colour, a good fit and a bargain — my tiny mother with the foolish cap of grey curls lurched from rack to rack leaning heavily on her walker, while I followed behind carrying our purses.

WHEN I WAS GROWING UP, MOM WOULD OFTEN HEAD DOWN-town to shop on Saturdays, leaving Dad in charge of us four kids. She'd tramp through stores for hours, on her feet until her legs ached, trying on clothes or imagining how something would fit one of us, anxious over the particulars of style, fit and price, trying to get everything just right. I knew the routine because sometimes my sister and I went with her: we'd take the 19 Kingsway bus, getting off on Hastings Street near Army and Navy, the first store we'd visit, trailing behind Mom as she bargain-hunted, continuing west to Fields, Woodward's, Woolworths and Eaton's. Our final foray would be to Hudson's Bay at the corner of Georgia and Granville, unless we had to double back after price checking.

If we were lucky, we'd finish by going to Clancy's for supper, where my sister and I would share an order of waffles topped with strawberries and whipped cream. "Better not tell the boys," Mom would say. "I don't know what Dad's got for them."

I could guess, because whenever she went on her own, Dad fixed our meal. He'd either heat up TV dinners, the food nicely separated in compartments, or else he'd make his specialty, chopped wieners in scrambled eggs. "Mmm, smells good!" he'd exclaim optimistically while I picked at stringy bits of egg clinging to bulging chunks of meat, wondering when Mom would get home.

Sometimes, she'd stop to have dinner and a glass of wine; as it got later and later, I'd begin to worry. It was a relief when she finally trudged through the kitchen door, complaining in a drained voice, "I thought that bus would never come." If she hadn't found any bargains, she'd snap at the sight of me: "I'm in no mood to be bothered." But when there was something to try on, no matter how tired, Mom would call me into her bedroom.

If the blouse or skirt or dress didn't pass muster, usually for being too big, "Oy," she'd groan, "I'll have to return it." I'd feel awful for causing Mom such trouble, responsible for the bad fit, as if I was small and skinny out of sheer meanness.

Mom's shopping trip before we visited my aunt on Vancouver Island was a triumph. Returning worn out and hauling several bags, she hurried down the hall to her room. When I slipped in to check if there was anything for me, Mom was sitting on the bed in a housecoat, her girdle and stockings hanging limply over the back of a chair. She was staring at a pale blue dress arranged at the end of the mattress alongside a crinoline and a hat topped with net that puffed up like a scrap of cloud, which she would wear on our travel day. "I hope I picked the right colour," she said, sounding doubtful.

My outfit had a nautical touch, in honour of the ferry we'd be taking: crisp white pedal pushers and a red and navy-blue striped top, with a cotton sun cap that had All Hands on Deck written across the front. I ran to my room to try everything on, racing back to show the perfect fit to Mom. She gave a creaky, exhausted smile, and I felt proud, as if it was me, not the outfit, that was the exact right size.

THE HOME NURSE'S SUGGESTION THAT MOM BEGIN THINKING about palliative care was angrily dismissed. "I'm not ready to die,"

Mom insisted. "Just get me into a seniors' residence." My sister and I accompanied her to look at a place she enthused over, but a few days later the nurse arrived at the condo, took one look at my mother and ordered an ambulance to take her to the hospital. "Hurry, you've got to meet me there," Mom said over the phone. "It's a terrible mistake."

The moment I arrived in the room where she was stretched out in bed — at the other end of the palliative care ward where Dad had taken his last breath less than a year earlier — she begged me to take her home. "If you were a good daughter, you'd do what I ask. You wouldn't leave me here."

The next morning, and for a few weeks after that, I fetched tea she could barely sip, food she couldn't swallow. "I have to build my strength up so they'll let me go home," she fretted, complaining loudly about how "that nurse, the dark one" kept her waiting for meals. "What are you worried about?" Mom snapped when I tried to hush her. "No one's listening." I apologized for her behaviour to the nurse, who put her hand reassuringly on my arm; like all the palliative care staff, she was an angel who would quietly care no matter what was thrown her way. Judging from her accent, the nurse was an immigrant, and looked about the same age as my grandmother had been when she first came to Canada after escaping Soviet Russia.

Grandma and her family had settled near Hines Creek, Alberta, where Grandpa and his brothers helped build Saint Pokrovsky Orthodox church in the 1930s. It's still standing, a log structure with three domes, each carrying high a Russian triple-barred cross. Mom worshipped there growing up, and my grandparents are buried in the church graveyard. We last paid our respects at their graves in the 1990s — Mom, my young daughter and me — when the three of us were in Hines Creek visiting her brother, Sam, before he passed on. Now, hoping to bring spiritual comfort, I fetched the icon of Mary and baby Jesus that had always hung on my parents' bedroom wall, but Mom paid it no attention. When the Russian priest with his long black beard came to see her in the palliative care ward, she didn't seem to notice, groaning and asking for help with bedsores.

I missed being with my mother at the moment of her death because I'd been dawdling at the grocery store, reluctant to head over to hear her latest complaints about the nurse, the food and probably me. On the way home, walking slowly in the March sun, my feet fell heavily on the pavement, as if the small incline was a mountain.

Unloading the food, I played my phone messages: there was just one, from the hospital, saying to come quickly. I ran all the way, heart and lungs at their limit as I burst into Mom's room. Instead of the usual reproaches for being even a few minutes late, there was only silence.

After my siblings arrived, we sat around Mom's deathbed, squabbling over funeral arrangements. That would have been Dad's way of putting it. "You kids stop your squabbling," he'd say when we were young. I left before anything had been decided, wanting to get back for my daughter, who'd be home from high school. Walking up the street, I was light-headed, giddy and disoriented. "I'm free!" cracked like thunder in my head, almost doubling me over with something that felt shockingly like relief, followed by a quieter bolt: "They're both gone now."

Then, nothing.

Emptiness.

THE FUNERAL TOOK PLACE AT HOLY RESURRECTION, AN Orthodox church where Mom had occasionally gone with one of her sisters. I sat at the front, my daughter beside me, along with my siblings and their families, everyone holding a small white candle. My eyes and nose streamed so much I used up my supply of Kleenex halfway through the service, clutching the last sodden tissue to the end.

At the cemetery, Mom's coffin was lowered into the earth on top of Dad's matching one, solid metal boxes chosen and paid for a decade earlier, not quite top-of-the-line, but close, a rare extravagance. Then everyone headed over for a buffet lunch at my parents' place, a sumptuous spread organized by my sister and a sister-in-law. The condo, though full of people eating and talking, felt empty without my parents. They'd hardly had time to enjoy their new home and now here we were, using their table, spilling food on their rug, sitting on their large plush couch.

I'd helped them buy the couch downtown at the Bay. Dad had dropped Mom and me off, saying he'd meet us in the furniture department after parking the car. We'd gone through the whole department, but Dad had still not shown up. "Where is he?" Mom kept fretting. "I bet he can't find parking." Which meant street parking because he'd never pay to use a lot.

When Dad arrived, he was limping so badly Mom said only, weakly, "Oy, Andy, where've you been?" Even the salesman was quiet. Dad sank down on the couch we'd already chosen, heavily, as if needing to take the weight off his bones. "It's nice and soft," he said, and didn't even ask the price.

That day at my mother's funeral lunch, I pushed myself up from the couch I still thought of as theirs, empty sandwich plate in hand. A relative I barely knew approached, saying how much he had enjoyed the church service. We chatted in the noisy room, and then his wife joined us. She asked what I did. "I'm a writer." "Oh, a waiter," she said. "No, a writer," I repeated. I had been slow to respond and she didn't hear the clarification, already turning to join another conversation. It was ridiculous how one small letter — an "r" that became an "a" — could recreate a life, but shocking, too, the easy inadvertent erasure of so much effort. My decades of devotion to writing about dance as a critic, historian and journalist — my calling, the activity that defined me — vanished, leaving the bare bones of a self. But I moved on, too, as we do at social gatherings, even, or especially, at funerals — smoothly, as if I knew the steps.

~

ON A TABLE IN MY LIVING ROOM, THERE'S A PHOTO FROM before my parents were my parents, when they were Andy and Zina, newlyweds. They're walking up Granville Street in downtown Vancouver, the neon lights of the Commodore bowling alley etched in the darkness behind them. Andy, carrying a small suitcase, strides forward in a suit and a wide tie with a splash of salmon-pink down one side, his hair a shining wave above his forehead. Zina wears a tight calf-length skirt and a striped fitted jacket that shows off her slender waist, a wisp of a hat nestled on top of soft curls, strappy grey heels on her feet. Her smile is wide and full of expectation, as if she's en route to adventure.

The photo is black and white, but I know the colours because the outfits were kept in my parents' bedroom closet, where I used to search through Mom's clothes for games of dress-up. She'd be busy in the kitchen or with my baby brother, and I'd sneak into the bedroom to try on one of her party dresses, sorting through the shoes jumbled on the floor to find the fancy ones.

Cocooned within her dress, its skirt trailing on the ground, stepping precariously in her high heels, I stumbled and fell, but it never hurt — my body was resilient, the joints well oiled, able to bend any which way with ease, to go with the flow that took me to the floor and then to quickly get up and clump around some more. In her finery I felt big and powerful, the way she seemed to be, the way I'd be all the time once I caught up to her and we were the same age — me and Mom, and Daddy, too, all of us knowing everything and getting everything just right.

My Renegade Body

IT CREPT UP, THE TROUBLE SWALLOWING. FOOD STUCK IN my throat no matter how much I'd drink to flush it down. A peculiar fullness settled in my upper chest, as if scraps from my breakfasts, lunches and dinners were piling up behind the breastbone. I kept burping, too, tiny eruptions that interrupted meals. When I went swimming with my teenage daughter, we'd take turns holding our breath underwater, the one above keeping watch in the crowded pool. "Hold on," I'd say, waiting for the spasms to stop before submerging.

In the middle of the night, I'd be pummelled by heartburn. The first few times, fearing a heart attack, I lay frozen in bed, prepared to call 911 if the pummelling got worse ... but how much worse? What if I waited too long? I dreaded making what might be an unnecessary fuss, and the fear and disruption it would create for my daughter, safely asleep.

My mother had complained of the same symptoms before her death a year earlier from cancer of the oesophagus. The coincidence was preposterous — what were my chances of getting the same cancer so soon after my elderly mother? Yet the signs were there and, like Mom, I ate less and less, until one day I bought a tiny pair of jeans, a sixteen-year-old's size, which the saleslady gushed over as if it was an accomplishment. I barely believed her then and definitely not the morning I tossed back my calcium pill and it scraped the sides of my throat, descending like a boulder bumping down a narrow canyon: I couldn't swallow them anymore, either. I saw myself shrinking smaller and smaller until, eventually, there'd be nothing left.

Caregiver's syndrome, my doctor suspected, but just to be sure, she sent me for the same test at the same hospital where I'd taken Mom. Now I was the one in a thin blue gown strapped upright onto a large machine, instructed to down a pasty liquid containing barium in one gulp before being spun round as x-rays were snapped of the barium's passage through my body. The results showed spasms in the upper oesophagus, probably stress-induced, definitely not cancer.

This was a relief; the stress would surely dissipate.

A few weeks later, I was back at the doctor's. For no apparent reason, with no connection to physical activity, my heart kept speeding up, beating faster and faster as if trying to build enough momentum to break free of bone and skin. Even as I sat in the clinic's packed waiting room, it went into such overdrive that I pushed my spine against the back of the chair as a buffer from the pounding, bullied by my own heart. Nothing unusual showed up on an EKG, so my doctor ordered an overnight Holter monitor. The moment the technician began attaching wires to my chest, I relaxed, feeling safe and cared for, my heart softening and slowing; I knew this test wouldn't show much, either.

A day after returning the monitor, as I lay flat on my back at the end of yoga class, my heart was racing again, thumping its distress. Listening to the gentle breathing of the peaceful bodies scattered around the room, I willed myself into stillness, wondering how so much could be going on inside without any outward evidence. The only clue, had anyone been looking, was my eyes, wired wide open.

My lungs were next, collapsing from the effort of climbing just two flights of stairs, curling together as if tightly wrapped in cling film. The previous summer, I'd hiked a mountain, a small one with a switchback, but still, I'd made it to the top and now I was panting as if two flights of stairs were Mount Everest. This led to more tests, exhaling into plastic tubes to assess lung capacity. "You could join the army!" the technician joked, because my lungs, as crafty and unreliable as my heart, behaved beautifully that day.

When I went in to discuss these latest results with my doctor, she reported that my lungs were fine, then dropped her head to say, "Maybe you should see a psychiatrist."

I'd had the same thought many times, but now that it was official medical advice, my heart began its furious beating, my lungs got tighter and smaller, and my throat constricted until I could barely croak, "Who?" The single syllable sounded in two sharp pieces, as if the word had broken in half as it struggled up my throat and out my weirdly twisted mouth.

"I don't know," she said uneasily, psychiatry clearly an unfamiliar last-ditch resort.

At home, not knowing where else to turn, I called a mental health emergency help line, heart and lungs quivering on high alert, electricity crashing through my veins. "Are you thinking of harming yourself?" the woman who answered asked. Since the answer was no — this was not an emergency situation — she couldn't offer any help, though she did explain that psychiatrists are medical doctors and, with a GP's referral, are covered in British Columbia by medicare, which was a huge relief.

Feeling like a fraud and not wanting to waste her time, I hung up, freeing the line for a more urgent caller. I was coping, not crazy, though my heart, lungs and blood continued to panic.

I phoned one of the two friends who knew what bad shape I was in and got her therapist's number. "Dr. B saved my life!" she said, unleashing a surge of hope he could do the same for me, and providing encouragement for the next step — explaining my situation to his receptionist, and for the next one — arranging a referral letter from my GP so my name could be added to Dr. B's waiting list. Making my mental health issues public, asking for support, was a crash course in humility: I wanted to be the kind of person who resolved things herself, I'd thought I was that kind of person.

Until recently, I had been managing reasonably well. This was despite having long ago diagnosed myself, after reading Dostoyevsky as a teenager, with brain fever, a vague neurological state of intense mental agitation and distress suffered by several of his characters. Everyone in his novels was buffeted by some form of extreme emotion, resulting in sudden fevers and other illnesses, or behaviour that was almost too exaggerated to believe, except it reminded me of my mother and a little of myself. I had taken this emotional excess to be an inherited Russian trait that simply had to be endured. Whenever my own brain fever descended, I got used to pushing it down into a hum of sadness only I could hear. It was easier with age, the intensity seeming to naturally flatten out into a garden-variety form of mild depression that often came and went, but wasn't so disruptive anyone needed to know. Only somehow, for the first time, my mental health was out in the open.

Over the nine months it took to move to the top of Dr. B's waiting list, most nights I was afraid to go to sleep, afraid of waking a few hours later with chest pain and the terrible worry about whether it was stupid or sane to not call 911. Or there would be that furious beating heart, with the world hurtling past faster than I could handle. I'd long given up coffee, tea, chocolate, wine, all possible contributors to the adrenalin rush that shot me bolt upright at three or four a.m. There I'd be, ready to ward off tigers and bears, and nothing more to do than walk my dog in the early hours of the morning.

~

JUST BEFORE TWO ON A MONDAY AFTERNOON, IN THE fifth-floor reception of the Kitsilano low-rise Dr. B shared with several businesses, I slid back into a soft leather couch, not quite long-legged enough to stop the slide, feeling much shorter than my five feet six-and-a-half inches. I flipped through the newspaper lying on the coffee table, worrying over what to talk about — I'd never been to a psychiatrist — when a slender man about my height and age glided in and said just one word, "Hello," firmly, in my direction. I pushed myself up as briskly as possible, trying to appear assured and collected and not crazy in front of the well-groomed receptionist, following Dr. B to his office. A few steps from his door, he stopped to let me pass so I entered first.

The small room was filled with a mahogany desk that faced the entrance and, at the other end, two sturdy leather armchairs placed directly opposite each other. Dr. B nodded at the chair that looked out on a large corner window, into which I settled, disappointed by the bland view of beige condominiums. Lightly dropping into his chair, Dr. B leaned back and said, "Tell me about yourself."

"Well," I fumbled, at a loss with such an open-ended question, the kind I would never use to begin one of the interviews I often conducted with dancers and choreographers for newspaper or magazine stories, or in post-show artist chats. I came to those prepared, having researched the person and their work beforehand, with a few questions ready to help ease us into a conversation. The generality of Dr. B's request was irritating; I wished I were in charge.

"I've recently become an orphan," I blurted.

Since I was nearly fifty, married for about a decade and long divorced, a mother myself, it was a ridiculous reply. Out of all the things I might have said, why this?

"My dad died from prostate cancer two years ago. Less than a year later, my mom died from cancer of the oesophagus." Then one more, making a third strike: "In between, my editor died, from pancreatic cancer."

Dr. B looked concerned, but didn't say anything.

"I write about dance," I said, to explain the editor: Lawrence Adams from Dance Collection Danse. He used to phone late at night from his home in Toronto to chat about our projects. When we launched my first book, on theatrical dance in early Vancouver, Lawrence called the evening before and asked what I was going to wear to the event, excited for me and for himself, too, having masterminded the whole thing.

"I'm a critic," I said. "I cover all kinds of theatrical dance. Writing about dance is my calling." Out loud, "my calling" sounded ludicrously grandiose, as if I were a nun and dance a religion; to give a more modest perspective, I added, "Dance is the underdog in the art world. It isn't taken seriously, even by other artists."

"Like psychiatry in the medical world," Dr. B said, cracking a smile. I did as well, appreciating how he had just levelled the ground between us despite the obvious fact that psychiatrists have more social and financial status than any kind of arts writer.

The friend who recommended him knew I'd appreciate his training in psychoanalysis. She's also a writer; we'd taken a course together using Freudian ideas to interpret Shakespeare, after which we'd both published pieces inspired by Freud. In mine, comparing Shakespeare's *The Winter's Tale* and a contemporary dance, *duo no. 2* by Montreal's Édouard Lock, I threw out Freudian jargon as if I'd found the precise key to both artworks. Much of the essay now seems glib, yet psychoanalytic theory helped me get beneath the surface of the art and into its depths.

I believe in Freud's unconscious, I told Dr. B, but not in all the details: I don't think a dream about walking up stairs necessarily stands for sex or that girls suffer penis envy. A modern Freudian, he nodded agreeably. Psychoanalytical studies were just one part of his training as a psychiatrist, he explained, adding that he could prescribe drugs if needed.

"Have you been in psychoanalysis yourself?" I asked, knowing this was a traditional requirement.

"Yes," Dr. B replied, sounding cautious. "I did undergo several years of analysis." He paused before adding, "There were family issues with my brother to resolve."

The admission was reassuring, further proof Dr. B wasn't going to put himself on a pedestal and pretend to be a perfectly functioning, all-knowing authority figure. Not that family issues were my main concern: it was my failing heart, lungs and throat that had landed me here. Claustrophobia, too, which was getting worse and making it harder to get around the city, harder to keep secret.

The last time I had been able to enter a public washroom was months ago, I told Dr. B. It was a cramped room in a restaurant, in a deserted corner by the kitchen. I had peed quickly, washed my hands, then — too anxious about getting out to take time drying them — pushed and twisted the door handle to release the lock mechanism. Nothing budged. I rattled the knob, banging it back and forth, heart pumping fast and furious like a cheap mechanical imitation. When the cylinder in the centre of the knob finally popped up — seconds later, though it seemed long enough to suffocate — I was sick with relief.

Public washrooms were relatively easy to avoid; elevators, less so. Whenever possible I took stairs instead, considering six or ten or even twelve flights good exercise. But now, given the state of my lungs … and sometimes there were no stairs … Or they were locked, like the ones in Dr. B's building, which meant I had to put myself at the mercy of electrical currents and mechanical connections, initiating a crisis of confidence in the material world — in its reliability, its responsiveness.

"I could send you to someone who would treat the symptoms," Dr. B said as our fifty minutes drew to a close. "Behavioural therapy is usually effective with claustrophobia. Or we could go deeper, though it would take much longer."

Being convinced of the safety of elevators did not strike me as a good idea. I'd already been trapped twice in one, the first time for an hour, in utter darkness, in a shabby Mexico City hotel where I had just arrived on holiday; the second was at work at Granada TV in Manchester, when a maintenance man helped me scramble out between floors. What if the third time the door never opened, or some crucial steel wire snapped and the elevator plunged to a deadly crash? Apparently they don't crash these days, there are safety devices in place, but what if those devices fail?

I opted to stay with Dr. B for in-depth treatment, every Monday at two.

We returned to the lobby together so he could show me the stairs, which were accessed by pressing a red button on the wall that un-locked the door. "But you'll have to keep taking the elevator to get here. Will you be all right with that?"

"Yes," I said, though I wasn't sure.

"Do you want me to come down with you now?"

"No, I'll be fine."

I ran down the stairs, past the locked doors on every landing (I checked), past the janitor's mop and pail, relieved when the very last door on the ground floor opened as easily as Dr. B promised it would.

Diving Lessons

THE FOLLOWING MONDAY, AFTER POSITIONING OURSELVES in the armchairs, Dr. B flipped to a new page in his notepad, scrawling my name across the top. He looked up expectantly, as if I was late for my cue. But he hadn't given one, so I sat quietly, staring out the window at row upon row of empty condo balconies, wanting him to take responsibility for the first move.

My immediate concern was leaving when the session was over. I pictured the stairwell I'd have to descend, with its five locked doors and the single unlocked one at the bottom. My safe exit depended on that ground floor door … but what if the doorknob jammed? What if the janitor accidentally locked it?

"Tell me about your childhood," Dr. B finally prompted.

Of course. That's where psychoanalysis starts. Only what could my childhood, on a quiet street on Vancouver's east side, have to do with the absurd physical breakdown that brought me here?

"I'm the second child, the second daughter," I said, figuring these were basics a therapist would want to know.

He nodded, and waited.

"I'm sure my parents were disappointed. They probably wanted a boy — one girl, one boy, it would have been perfect."

He nodded, and waited.

"A year and a half later, Mom did have a boy, and then another one. So it was just right in the end — two boys, two girls."

At that moment, three men strolled onto one of the balconies, each clutching a disposable white coffee cup that dangled over the edge of the rail on which they leaned. In unison, the men lifted their arms to drink; the cups, catching the sun, shone beautiful and bright like the bellies of seabirds.

While Mom was away in hospital for the birth of my youngest brother, a French maid looked after us. The way I see her in my mind — in a short black dress, with a frilly white apron — can't be accurate; do such maids even exist except in old Hollywood movies? Certainly not in our lives: our bungalow on Vimy Crescent, named to commemorate Canadians lost at Vimy Ridge during World War I, was in a subdivision developed in 1948 as low-rental housing for veterans; Dad's World War Two navy service must have qualified us to live there.

I didn't tell Dr. B about Vimy Crescent, the memories flickering by in fragments: the French maid laughing as I jumped on my parents' bed; the strip of garden filled with snapdragons I thought would bite off my fingers if I got too close; a match flaring up in my hand as I stood alone in the front yard. Fire looked friendly and bright when Mom lit her cigarettes, but suddenly its fierceness and heat was revealed. I dropped the match into the dirt that edged the sidewalk and ran inside, pushing my bad behaviour into the pit of my stomach, hoping no one would ever know I had almost burned down the house.

Did that really happen, did I really think that? Mom smoked occasionally for a few years; had she already started at Vimy Crescent? Would a four-year-old's fingers be nimble enough to light a matchstick?

I stared at my hands nestled in my lap, the skin snaked with the maze of thick turquoise veins Mom had hated. "What's wrong with your hands?" she demanded the morning Dad, my young daughter and I visited the hospital after she'd been temporarily capsized by a stroke. "Nothing," I'd said, drawing them away from the side of the bed where she lay and crossing my arms to hide the large ropey veins that mapped a vital journey of lifeblood.

Dr. B, a shadow presence in well-pressed shirt and trousers, was waiting for me to speak. I forced my head up but, avoiding eye contact, turned toward the window. The balcony where the three men had stood was deserted except for a single coffee cup left behind on the ground, looking small and dumpy in the shade.

A flash of movement higher up turned out to be a workman on a rooftop. One false move and he'd fall to the earth. My stomach clenched and then it tumbled in that sickening way it does at danger — not because the man had fallen, but because I had, back into the past. It was like drowning, like water seeping into my head, my stomach, my arms and legs, but when I opened my mouth to gasp for air, words rushed out.

DESPITE SWIMMING LESSONS AS A CHILD, I NEVER LEARNED to dive properly. It was easier to plug my nose, shut my eyes and jump in feet first. After the descent, there would be such stillness at the bottom waiting for buoyancy to kick in. During the anxious pause before the reversal of forces, it seemed likely my life would end submerged at the bottom of a body of water with its own mysterious urges.

Only with Dr. B, in his quiet corner office, did I finally learn the style and mechanics of an efficient dive, arms outstretched into prayer hands that broke the surface and took me headlong underwater, eyes wide open. The place where we practised was in the river of sadness that flowed through the centre of the house on Clarendon Street where my family moved when I was five. Each week, I plunged into its cold unwelcoming depths to retrieve my childhood — the difficult parts, half-hidden in the riverbed, which interested Dr. B. As he waited patiently above the surface, I brought him memories of doing this, hearing that, of feeling and thinking and being in the non-stop rush of those early years when everything was new, when every adult seemed a free and powerful being in charge of the world, in utter contrast to myself. In the memories I lifted and carried, dragged and pushed to the surface, two people were always either there or not there — Dad, who was often away at work, and Mom, who never was. Often my older sister and two younger brothers appeared, but my parents and I were at the centre of my life on Clarendon Street.

It usually took only a few strokes to reach the primary source of the river: my mother's tears, which flowed easily in response to life's provocations. On a rainy day, I might track mud into the kitchen and Mom would be furious, yelling at me for being such a bad girl, yelling about what bad ungrateful children we all were, too lazy to clean up after ourselves, too lazy to help around the house, and Andy, our dad, was no better, never home when she needed him. She would shout as if I was miles away, as if she couldn't see me standing right there in front of her. Even once I was curled up on my bed, trying not to hear, Mom would keep shouting. Hunched over the sink preparing carrots and potatoes for stew, she might sob that her hands were red and sore from scraping the vegetables; crying, too, about how she had to cut out black bits in the potatoes till nothing was left, how Dad must have bought them on special, he was always looking for a bargain, he never bought what she wanted, he never listened to her, we never listened, nobody did. Her anger had to run its course, which ended only when her throat was sore, a few last hard barks sounding a grudging defeat.

In the middle of one of my mother's storms, I might try to calm her, using what I thought was a reasoning grown-up voice, but she couldn't hear, not with the river roaring between us. I'd end up shouting as well, but she paid no attention, as if I was too insubstantial to be seen or heard.

"I'm at the end of my tether!" my pretty dark-haired mother would scream, coughing in spasms of fury as her throat seized up. There we'd stand on opposite riverbanks, and my throat, too, would constrict, though I had barely hollered.

A crazy darkness kept welling up inside Mom, spilling out into all our lives. I thought it was because she was just plain mean, and hated her for it.

"OY," MY MOTHER WOULD GROAN IN MY EAR DURING THER-
apy, a long guttural sound that seemed to erupt from the bowels of the
earth, just like it did when she was alive. "What are you talking about
that for?" I'd hear my father's voice, coming down from on high as it
had when I was a child and he was God and John Wayne rolled into
one, booming his saintly refrain: "If you don't have anything good to
say, don't say anything at all." Even though Dr. B wanted me to talk
about all that, to say anything at all, I hated being the black sheep in
the family, the only one who would be so disloyal, doubting myself,
questioning each memory, as if the truth lay out there with someone
else, anywhere but inside me.

Instead of relaxed private conversations with Dr. B, every session
felt like a public accounting before a judge and jury. The fear I wasn't
getting things right sent shivers through my body; I'd grab my coat
and wrap it tightly round. Why did they matter so much, the things
I said? "My mother's version would be different," I'd insist. Or my
father's or sister's or brothers'.

"You're the opposite of a narcissist," Dr. B commented early on.
"You try to see everything from other people's points of view."

At first I took this as a compliment, flooded with relief at not
being a narcissist. Until, over the course of our sessions, I discovered that the opposite was to have no centre, only a void from which
I somehow had to find my voice and send it out to fill the room
with "me." I'd tell myself that Dr. B was well paid to listen to me
talking about me, but it didn't lessen the anxiety. My throat would
turn into a desert, and I'd gulp from the water bottle kept handy in
my purse. Sometimes a boa constrictor wrapped itself around my
windpipe, preventing me from saying a word. If I tried to put Dr. B
in the hot seat by asking about his life, he'd answer briefly and then
the waiting game returned: our silent sitting until I put myself out
there again.

When I saw Dr. B's eyes drooping, his jaw gaping open, I apologized for being a bore and bringing up the same old story.

"Some things have to be gone over several times," he said earnestly. "Yawning isn't a value judgement, it's just that I listen to people all day and might get tired."

The switch flipped then, the one that put me on his side, inhabiting the situation from his point of view: worrying over how he had to listen to me, to the multitude of me's who traipsed through his door every day, every working hour, spewing our dull and ordinary pain.

Another time I apologized for shouting. Dr. B told me it was okay to raise my voice, which, he said, hadn't been that loud. "I've never seen you angry before," he added.

"Other people get angry in therapy?" I'd said in surprise.

"Well, yes, they might express anger sometimes." Even, apparently, toward him, if he forgot something they'd previously shared or if they caught him yawning. He made it sound as if it was all right for them to do that, and it would be all right for me to, as well.

From that point on, I tried not to track Dr. B's reactions so closely — to not notice when his pen moved across his notepad, when it slowed and when it stopped (was he bored again?) — and instead to focus fully on me, on growing up by the river that ran through the house on Clarendon Street. I tried not to worry about Dr. B, to not feel obligated to be interesting or to imagine what it was like to be forever listening to other people's unhappy lives.

BY THE END OF THE FIRST YEAR, MY HEART HAD STOPPED TRYING to pound its way out of my chest, my brain no longer crashed into action in the early hours of the morning and I could sleep through the night. The words required by therapy were so concrete, relentlessly defining and pinning down the past, and yet they anchored me to the world.

By the end of the second year, I could swallow large vitamin pills without choking and, on good days, step into elevators.

Week after week, as I dragged out the childhood conversations and events still taking up space in my head, Dr. B listened intently, as if

each one were of Shakespearean proportion, making notes, occasionally offering a few thoughts. The most banal domestic drama could
fuel insight, shared quietly in his straightforward style. His drive to
interpret these memories was connected to my drive as a critic to
interpret dance, both of us invested in making meaning through close,
conscientious attention to our material.

Dr. B's interpretations were shaped by a keen belief in the im-
portance of "the primary caregiver" in a child's early years. In our
single-family home, like most others in my time and place, this meant
Mom; our daily interactions were my major source of information
about the world, how it worked and how I fit within it. Yet Dad, despite being away at work during the helter-skelter childhood days, was
another primary caregiver and I wished he were present in therapy
more often.

As it was — because of psychotherapy's expectations, or society's,
or mine — encounters with my mother played the major part in our
sessions. There had been so many days, so many opportunities to have
things go wrong; my memory banks were filled with the minutiae of
our conflicts. Like the time in grade four when I wrote her a letter.

Neither of us had gone anywhere, but whenever the river raged it
was as if we were miles apart. She was resting in bed, I was down the
hall in my bedroom reading — I was such a good reader, even a great
one, trekking to the library every Saturday, returning an armful of
books and choosing another load for the week ahead. *Anne of Green
Gables* or a Nancy Drew mystery were my escape from the day's skir-
mishes, but, on this occasion, I couldn't concentrate. This is when the
brainwave struck: I would explain myself by writing Mom a letter, so
heartfelt she couldn't fail to understand me. With that would come
her support, which was the necessary ground of my existence and
would resolve all anxieties over my place in the family constellation
that was the world.

My behaviour was always making her mad. Maybe I gagged over
lumps in the Cream of Wheat at breakfast and then, at dinner,

crabbed because a sibling got the biggest piece of Mom's beloved cinnamon-and-nutmeg-scented apple pie. I wanted to explain how Cream of Wheat made me sick to my stomach, that I hadn't deliberately taken so long to eat it, and to say how it wasn't fair I never got the biggest piece of pie, I was always second or third or fourth for everything.

"Oy," Mom sighed when I handed her the letter. "I'm about to start dinner." Quickly unfolding the sheet of paper, she glanced over it. "What are you talking about? I don't have time for this."

There it was out in the open, one of those insistent memories, featuring nothing more than a self-centred child and an overworked mother. Sunk deep into my armchair in my therapist's office, retreating into an embarrassed silence, it was all I could do to breathe, to exist no further than in the slow intake and expulsion of air. Trying to be present with intelligent adult "now," free of stupid childish "then."

"You used writing as a means to communicate," Dr. B mused quietly.

With those few words, the memory shifted and gained new significance: it was no longer about feeling invisible and unheard, but an expression of my drive to be a writer. Dr. B granted agency to the nine-year-old who wrote the letter and was still present somewhere deep inside, as are all the incarnations of self, each one building a layer dependent on those below.

It's not that I thought of myself as a writer back then; I didn't think of myself as anything, or of what I was going to be when I grew up. A stewardess? A teacher? Hopefully pretty like Barbie, with lots of outfits and lots of dates to wear them on. Mostly, I just wanted to get to adulthood, so I could be my own person, with no parents or big sister to boss me around. At school, it was enough that each writing assignment was an opportunity to put myself down on paper and get the attention of the beautiful women who were my first teachers: Miss Taylor and Miss Wright, lavishing gold and silver stars on my stories and reports. Miss Chitrenky, too, a goddess in cat's-eye glasses and hastily pinned French roll. Once, as she quietly patrolled the aisles while we worked at our desks, she put her hand over mine to stop my nervous fidget. The warmth of her touch inspired my best efforts during the entire fourth-grade school year.

"You wanted your mother to listen, to see you and show her approval and love," Dr. B said in his usual calm voice. "This is natural, all children want attention and most parents give it. A child on a bike shouts, 'Look at me!' and the mother looks and smiles. Your mother didn't make room for you to be seen and heard, she didn't know how."

That day, in the hothouse of therapy, those mundane truths formed a finely wrought key that opened up another time and space. My world collapsed and expanded at the same time, and in this maelstrom the child caught up to the mother, just like my younger self had expected would happen one day. In a flash, I was back with Mom on Clarendon Street at the river's edge, only it was different now: we were two adults standing together, each of us doing the best we could.

In this altered scenario, my mother's voice sounded different — not just angry, but despairing. I could hear deeper into the nagging litany of complaint to what she was holding back: a scream as the river inside her rose, as it leaked out her mouth and nose and eyes, across the kitchen and through our house. In that scream lay all the dinners, all the lunches and breakfasts, all the children and all their demands, with no time for anything above and beyond the daily grind. Instead, the unexpected loneliness of the self-sufficient family unit, of being confined to the enclosed space of her own home, the anguish of the Canadian dream of domestic bliss that ended up being just one more needy child with one more childish dilemma to resolve.

My Mother's Renegade Body

SOME DAYS ON CLARENDON STREET, WHEN MY MOTHER'S torrent of words wouldn't stop, there had been one sure way to get her attention. "You're crazy!" I'd shout, circling a finger round in the air at the side of my forehead to suggest scrambled brains. Her face would crumple for an instant before she returned with even more fury to her litany of life's inadequacies and betrayals. I'd run outside to hide behind the house, by the strip of dirt where I once planted green beans, Mom's voice a faint roar in the distance.

When I was older, I discovered the reason the taunt was so effective: as a young woman, my mother had spent time in a psychiatric facility. I'm not sure why she confided her secret to me; it might have been because of the first-year psychology courses I was taking at college, which made me seem smarter and more mature in her eyes. Or maybe she knew I was good at keeping things to myself, and I never did tell anyone until after her death.

Her confession came out of the blue, when I was fussing in front of the full-length mirror that hung on my parents' bedroom door, trying to decide what to wear to classes that afternoon. Mom was resting, stretched out in bed in her housecoat. I knew my indecision would be getting on her nerves, but nothing fit or went together. I tried another top, another pair of pants, craning my neck to see each outfit from every angle, to see me from every angle, because I was never sure if it was the clothes or myself that didn't fit. Instead of groaning in irritation — What was taking so long? Why didn't I get going? Wasn't I going to be late? — she began talking.

After finishing high school, Mom said, making it sound like an accomplishment, though it was something I took for granted, she signed up for a secretarial course. I could tell she was proud of that, too, and of travelling to Fairview for the course, or was it Grande Prairie? I can't remember, but somehow she got there every day from the family farm outside Hines Creek. Training in office skills was a major move away — away from the farm and the family — but also toward something — her own future on her own terms.

She had a flair for shorthand and typing, and moved to the city, to Vancouver, in search of opportunities to use her new skills. Mom got "a good job" at the Royal Bank, the branch on Hastings Street at the foot of Granville, with impressive marble floors and a high arched ceiling.

"I was going out with this fellow, we were supposed to get married... He jilted me. I don't know what happened, maybe he found someone else."

The pain in her voice sounded very present, as if she hadn't stopped thinking of him; what about Dad, I worried? I was sitting on her bed now, by her feet, and hardened myself, fearing a betrayal. But the story took a new direction.

"I had a bit of a nervous breakdown," Mom continued, sounding apologetic. "I was in Riverview, they gave me shock treatment."

I knew about Riverview, a mental health facility, or, as we called such places as kids, the loony bin, and had just read about shock treatment — electroconvulsive therapy, or ECT, in which electrical currents are passed through the brain in order to trigger a brief seizure. This wasn't in psychology class, but in a literature course, where we were reading Ken Kesey's *One Flew Over the Cuckoo's Nest*. Kesey's sensational portrayal of ECT as a cruel, barbaric practice that turned unruly patients into zombies had filled me with sympathy for the eccentrics and misfits he depicted being forced to undergo it. Now that group included my own mother.

"It was nothing much," Mom said when I asked what shock treatment was like. "Everybody makes such a big fuss about things nowadays."

We sat closer, not literally, but softening our boundaries, becoming porous so the same river of sadness that ran inside my mother trickled inside of me. Apparently the songs were true — a woman could go crazy if the man she loved didn't love her — and that was the end of it.

When I told Dr. B about the ECT, he was keen to know more. Since Mom was no longer here, I phoned one of her sisters. After "that man" left her, Aunt Kay said, Mom stopped going to work and wouldn't leave her apartment. When she fell behind on the rent, the landlord stepped in and called Riverview for help.

"I was still living in Hines Creek," Aunt Kay recalled, "but there was no one else to get Zina, so I hurried to Vancouver and brought her home. I don't know what happened, but it wasn't serious. The doctor told me, 'There's nothing wrong with your sister, she's just a spoiled brat.'"

When he heard this, Dr. B pointed out the phrase didn't sound like something a doctor would say. Also, if it were true, why would ECT have been prescribed? Perhaps that's how the family preferred to remember the incident, he suggested: Zina was spoiled, as the youngest often are, but not crazy.

I don't know the exact nature of my mother's symptoms: the hospital records have been lost, and her own description of a nervous breakdown was a generic diagnosis for women that was typical of the era, suggesting a physical problem of nerves. Hers were always delicate, needing protection from the onslaught of daily life, considered a very feminine weakness. In Dr. B's opinion, Mom must have been severely depressed to warrant the ECT.

Though I am not convinced of its safety, the procedure is very different today, and Dr. B believes it to be a legitimate option in certain situations. Whatever the case for ECT, that was it as far as professional help for my mother went: Zina, the young woman who had been unable to step outside the confined space of her apartment — unable to move, unable to eat, whose body felt heavy and oppressive — had to pull herself together as best she could.

She returned to Vancouver, on her own again until meeting Andy. I had never thought to ask how they met, and they didn't reminisce about their first meeting the way some couples do. Zina turned twenty-eight the month after their marriage, old for a bride then, she once told me, embarrassed. They would go on to raise four children, my mother believing that if no one knew about that awful time, her "bit of a breakdown" would not have to be part of our family story.

But it was, of course. I had no choice but to get used to the river that ran through our house. It was as much a fixture as the fancy chandelier in the dining room or the door that closed off the kitchen by sliding out of the wall. Or the bathtub that I could stretch right out in when I was small. Floating on my back, alone and perfectly quiet, the still warm water was nothing like the river's sad, turbulent flow.

An Interpretation of Dresses

AFTER THREE YEARS OF THERAPY, MY BODY WAS BACK ON my side, working for and not against me. Breath returned to my lungs and my vocal cords stopped constricting at the slightest stress. I could climb stairs and small mountains again; I could talk to Dr. B without coughing and choking. My voice felt supported. It had been ages since I'd heard my mother groan during a session or my father advise me not to say anything. I could submerge into the past more deeply, talk about "all that" more freely.

"I'm trying to understand the world through your eyes, to feel what it's like to be you," Dr. B said more than once. The foundation of his understanding was the family unit and the dance we created, step by step, over many years, based on relationships and behaviour that became so familiar they were taken for granted. Like gravity, the family dance seemed inevitable: I was doing what I had to do, all that I could do, and so was everybody else. Dr. B was helping to reveal those long-established patterns, and new, more productive ones finally seemed possible. At about the four-year mark, I reduced our sessions to biweekly.

Then one morning I woke to a familiar darkness inside. A shroud muffled every thought and feeling, and was still there a few days later when I sat opposite Dr. B in his office.

My first words were an apology for feeling "a little depressed," definitely an understatement. "I often feel a bit down before my period begins," I said.

"What happened?" Dr. B asked, ignoring my excuse.

"Nothing in particular."

It was the best answer I could come up with, having no idea what triggered this latest attack. But, as if I had said "something" not "nothing," Dr. B waited expectantly and I plunged into our session, pinpointing the start of the depression to the drive home with a friend at the end of an afternoon. The air had become heavy; I was ill at ease and wanted to be alone.

He nodded, again looking expectant, and a description of the afternoon poured out, starting with our decision to do some shopping after lunch. As if I knew where my words were heading, I explained that in the first store we visited my friend spotted a gorgeous black dress, then, because it was too small for her, insisted I try it on. When I emerged from the changing room, she groaned good-naturedly, wishing it would fit her like that. The salesclerk pointed out the price tag, marked fifty percent off. They both said how good the dress looked on me, how good I looked in it. I could see from my reflection in the full-length mirror they were right: we were a beautifully integrated unit of fabric and flesh.

Alone in the changing room, stepping carefully out of the skirt's immaculate expanse, I wondered how often I would wear such a formal dress. It would need a lot of ironing and, if I gained a mere ounce, the zipper wouldn't close. Focused on practicalities, remembering the other seldom worn dresses already in my closet, I pulled on my own clothes and returned the dress to the rack. My friend's face shut down with disappointment; so did the salesclerk's. The euphoria of being the exact right size — the perfect size for the perfect dress — trickled away.

MOM USED TO MAKE DRESSES FOR MY SISTER AND ME, which always fit perfectly because if they didn't, she would take in a seam or move a button. My first was green chiffon, for my ninth birthday. The following summer's yellow sundress had delicate spaghetti straps she said were "very sophisticated, really for older girls." Wearing it, I felt sophisticated like the dress, like an older, smarter, more attractive girl. Once the sewing became too much of a chore, Mom would exhaust herself shopping for store-bought dresses, proud of her great finds at bargain prices.

Her last find for me was white, with blue piping, a twenty-eighth-birthday present. Sleeveless, with a tight bodice and flared skirt, it was exactly the right size, though too formal and fitted to be something I'd choose myself. "Except for the colour, it was similar to that black dress I tried on," I said.

Even without Dr. B's keen glance, it was obvious the coincidence — a white dress that transforms into a black one — was significant.

"I only wore the white dress to go out with my family. My parents seemed to like me in it."

"You wore it to please them," Dr. B said, "just as you considered buying the other dress to make your friend and the saleslady happy."

His simple statement, weaving together past and present, revealed connective tissue between two events despite their huge separation in time. It meant my depression wasn't random, but part of a larger pattern of behaviour, suggesting a soothing sense of order to which I clung. Depression can feel so big and deep and inevitable, as if it carries existential truth, and yet this time it had been caused by a mere dress. I left Dr. B's office relieved at finding this surely very manageable trigger.

Minutes later, descending the stairs, subtext wormed its way into consciousness: I was the kind of person who worries about the opinion of others. This became the sorry refrain playing in a loop in my head as I drove home following the familiar route — through the roundabout and the four-way stop, bumping along in the 12th Avenue traffic, stuck at the inevitable red lights. Even though my father and mother were both dead and gone, even though I was an independent middle-aged woman, I was still as driven to please — if not them anymore, then whoever happened to pass by.

I would never be free of my parents' influence. Our relationship remained a source of psychic energy I couldn't seem to mature beyond, the need to please was too deeply embedded: not just in my interactions with other people, but also in the creative drive I began for the first time to question. My work as a writer was apparently no more than a way to gain approval, a stupidly onerous way.

OVER A LIFETIME, I HAD NEVER TIRED OF THE MANY FORMS DANCE can take, or its many functions as art, entertainment, social activity, spiritual expression or simply a way to stay fit. As a dancer, then as a writer, I was intrigued by it all, but especially by the aspect of art. Since my byline had first appeared in the mid-eighties in a few pieces for a now-defunct London magazine called *New Dance*, I had never doubted the worthiness of artistic discussion.

The expressive qualities and technical strengths of individual dancers were so fascinating, and, for a writer, there was the additional need to tease out the presence of the choreographer, to distinguish the dancer from the dance and find something interesting to say about both. The intensely subjective nature of experiencing art had to be acknowledged: in the huddle with friends and acquaintances at intermission, the variety of their often passionate responses made that subjectivity obvious, as did the mix of reviews later in the media. The challenge was to try and see a choreographic work as objectively as humanly possible in order to develop accurate and fair-minded description. That description, whatever its limitations, had to add up to something, it had to draw out the meaning and intentions of the choreography, and it had to evoke my own actual experience that night in the theatre, leading to the inevitable evaluation — the judgement that many contemporary critics, including myself, prefer to avoid, at least when it is thumbs down.

The need to do all this with enough style to draw readers in, and to satisfy an editor's desire for clear, highly readable copy, had kept me engaged over and over again — until that session in therapy when ego, not aesthetic truth, appeared to be the real driver.

With bewildering speed, my usual eagerness to be in front of dancing bodies devolved into little more than a bad habit, the immersion into a choreography's shapes, colours and sounds no longer straightforward and consuming. Suddenly I was in it for the money, but when I protested the low fee for a current assignment — a newspaper obituary on a prominent choreographer — my editor's only response was that at least obituaries were better read than the arts pages. My typically small readership seemed shameful now, too. The bubble of devotion, the belief that dance mattered in and of itself, had burst.

I became discerning over what shows to attend; "discerning" is how I described it to myself, but really it was reluctance to risk a night at the theatre. I would estimate the likelihood of being bored, which happened more frequently. Staying up late to finish an overnight review, instead of being absorbed by the play of words, I wanted to go to bed. The incessant research demanded by writing wore on me: there was always more to know, a new wave of enthusiastic people and ideas to explore. As for slogging over another profile or feature, the prospect of learning about yet another artist's life, transcribing the interview and then writing and rewriting, filled me with dread.

Psychotherapy had gone too far, exposing the petty motivation that got me out of bed each morning, offering nothing to replace it. Now what was I supposed to do with my life?

I kept finding excuses to cancel my sessions with Dr. B, but couldn't bring myself to actually quit. I wanted to give up the crutch of writing, too, resenting my dependence on it to make a living and to connect to the world. There had to be something else, something outside the same straitjacketed behaviour, the same narrow script — a way to be a different kind of person, a different kind of writer. This intense dissatisfaction landed me in memoir, an intimate form that has always been important to me as a reader. Without the driver of dance, though, each word came slowly, with mind-numbing struggle, as if I were barely literate.

After I had slogged through and made some small progress, I mentioned this new territory to Dr. B. "That's great," he said, turning those two words into an anthem of interest and support.

I had formed a writing group with a couple of friends, I said. In his careful minimalist way, Dr. B nodded. Attuned by then to the subtleties of his responses, I remember clocking the force with which his head bobbed up and down, the keen way he looked right at me. *Dr. B nodded enthusiastically*, I should have written.

"This is very different for you," he'd mused, "telling your story instead of someone else's."

"I couldn't have tackled memoir before," I'd said, meaning before therapy.

"Being able to write about yourself is a sign of presence."

I never discussed with Dr. B the complications of subtext, which had revealed the danger of therapy: it can tell you more than you want to know about yourself. Today when I am in the theatre for a story or review about dance, making that imaginative leap across the footlights into a heightened artistic reality feels more and more like a blessing.

Or like magic. As a critic and member of the audience, I am safely in my seat, scribbling in my notebook, and yet, swept into the action onstage, I am also up there dancing in those fantastic imaginative ways. On really good evenings — when I am in good shape and the choreography soars — the dance and I are in such close partnership it's like a dream of metamorphosis, in which a simple fall can transform to become freedom and flight.

Now and Now

IT TOOK FIVE YEARS OF THERAPY BEFORE I FELT READY TO stop seeing Dr. B. He suggested monthly meetings "just in case," but, tired of being a patient, I wanted a clean break. I considered asking for a copy of the notes he took each week — he told me once I was entitled to read them — but in the end decided not to view my life through a therapist's jargon.

I missed our sessions, though, and at the same time and day attempted to establish a yoga practice at home. While time flew by at my two-hour Iyengar yoga class, all I could manage on my own was maybe a quarter hour, each minute creeping reluctantly forward as I raced through every pose.

At one solo practice, I folded my yoga mat next to a wall in order to run through the preparation for a headstand; I never went up on my own, needing someone to spot me in the precarious act of getting off my feet and onto my head. Kneeling, I laced my fingers together, bent forward and formed a V on the floor with my forearms, plunking the top of my head down below the apex. Hoisting my bum into the air, I walked my feet toward my head. I used to easily scramble into headstands as a kid, and just as I wondered where the paralyzing fear had come from, there I was — upside down, legs aloft.

With a rush like wind at my back, I felt again what it was to be a girl exploding into headstands, somersaults and wobbly cartwheels. At the same time, as a fifty-something woman standing on her head negotiating a long-lost relationship with gravity, there was a hush, a concentration of energy. Both times were very present, and I was very present in both times.

II

Clarendon Street

THE FIRST TIME WE VISITED OUR NEW HOME, THERE WAS nothing to see, just a giant hole in the ground. For the basement, Dad said. "Where you can play when it rains," Mom added. Dad pointed out where the kitchen would be, and the dining room next to it. With a wave of his hand, he conjured up a bedroom for my two younger brothers and then another one for my big sister and me. The primary school where I would start kindergarten was down the street. "It's so close, you can walk there by yourself," said Mom.

A few months later, when we returned, a one-storey house stood where the hole had been, a house with green wooden siding on the bottom and white plaster on top. And an address: 5211 Clarendon Street. Our address. A wild rose bush grew by the back stairs we climbed to enter through the kitchen door, carrying our boxes and bags across the sparkling linoleum. This back staircase, painted the same pastel green as the house, would be our usual entrance; only the mailman, Jehovah's Witnesses, the Fuller Brush man and special guests used the front stairs, which had a fancy wrought-iron handrail.

Our new house was filled with treasures. A chandelier glittered above the dining room table and a painting, *Blue Boy*, hung near the sliding door that could disappear into the wall or be pulled out to close off the kitchen. In the living room, a small brush, shovel and poker were placed neatly in a row by the fireplace. There was a painting of a ballerina in a long white tutu above the dresser in my parents' room; her arms, raised to frame her face, made a circle like the ones drawn around the heads of Mary and baby Jesus in the icon on the wall above the bed. A basket containing every shade of thread rested on the sewing machine, beside a tin filled with buttons I could plunge my hands into, searching for favourite colours and lining up matching sets. Each room was a playground of domestic architecture, of furniture and fixtures that made ideal hiding spots during hide-and-seek: under the kitchen table, inside the dirty clothes closet, behind the pink shower curtain.

In the hall, a wrought-iron railing marked off a stairwell leading into the basement. On rainy days, just like Mom had said, that's where we played. The expanse of cement floor, lit by bare bulbs hanging from the rafters, was empty except for several structural beams and a couple of trunks containing old clothes. Until Dad built a bedroom for the boys and a TV room down there, it was the perfect place for tag: we could run the entire width and breadth of the house, neatly shifting direction or recoiling a shoulder or hip to avoid whoever was It, dashing to safety. But never so far and so safe you were no longer in the game.

At one end of the basement, a furnace regularly banged into action, sending hot air via a series of ducts through the house. The room I shared with my sister was directly above; I'd hear the motor rev up while lying in our bed. It was Mom and Dad's old bed, and the mattress sagged in the middle so we'd roll toward each other during the night.

The headboard had three compartments, a large middle one to share and a smaller section of our own at each end. Mine displayed toys and jewellery, like my lamb brooch, the fur studded with pearls. Not real pearls — and not the real Gainsborough *Blue Boy* or a real crystal chandelier — but I was hardly aware of the distinction between real and pretend, or that it mattered.

At bedtime, after Mom turned off the light, she'd tell us to go straight to sleep. "I don't want any funny business," Dad would add if he happened to pass by. As soon as we were alone, stretched out side by side in bed, one of us would quietly chant: "Do you want to...?" That was the cue for the other to spell out the response, each letter sung like a note in a snappy jazz tune: "P-L-A-Y." New to spelling, I would be giddy with power.

P-L-A-Ys were epic. In one, my sister and I held our dolls, Betsy and Baby Sue, close as we travelled on a large ship in the middle of the ocean. A violent storm left us stranded in a lifeboat tossed about in huge waves. When my doll, Baby Sue, fell overboard, I jumped into the icy water, shrieking, to save her.

"What's going on in there?" boomed Dad from the hallway.

Grabbing Baby Sue, I scrambled back into bed. Dad pushed open the door, and I shut my eyes and held my breath, pretending to be asleep in the jumble of sheets and blankets.

ON WEEKDAY MORNINGS, MOM COOKED SUNNY BOY OR OAT-meal for breakfast, or Cream of Wheat we'd douse with brown sugar. Weekends, she'd be at the stove making stacks of pancakes we topped with cottage cheese and melted butter, or with maple syrup. Not real maple syrup, I know now: maple flavoured. Not real butter, either — margarine, which we called butter.

Or else she'd fry bacon and eggs, hot grease snapping at her arms. Some mornings, unable to bear the trace of slime on the sunny-side-up yolk, I'd be the last one at the table, forbidden to leave until my plate was empty. "What's taking you so long? You're in my way," Mom would say as she shoved things back into the fridge in the corner behind me. "This kitchen's too small!"

As Mom cleared plates and cutlery, then attacked the sink full of dirty dishes, the kitchen did feel crowded, though there was just me at the table, choking down the last of the egg.

The bathroom was also too small, Mom said, and cluttered. "Can't you kids pick up after yourselves?" There was only one hook on the door and one rack on the wall, so towels were thrown about, and the counter by the sink was strewn with odds and ends: a Bazooka Joe comic that came folded around bubble gum, forgotten socks and undershirts. I'd sweep everything aside before climbing up to reach the cabinet crammed with Mom's beauty potions, upending bottles of nail polish to watch the thick bright reds and oranges sluggishly drip down.

Running almost the length of one wall, which was lined with pink tiles, was a dazzling white enamel tub so big I could lie back and float like in a swimming pool, only at home there were no kids splashing water in my eyes. Once I grew a little, if I stretched right out, the tip of my head touched one end, my toes the other, as if the tub was made for me. I'd luxuriate in being the exact right size until an urgent knocking on the door meant someone needed to pee, and Mom wanted to know what I'd locked myself in for. Then the house was too small for me, too, with only one bathroom for the six of us.

The house in which I lived was mutable, spacious and inviting one minute, cramped and crowded the next. This duality never surfaced clearly in my mind, both realities existing by turn in a world that was unstable, each incarnation so convincing I fell for it every time.

THE DAY I WAS FINALLY BIG ENOUGH FOR SCHOOL, I WORE my new plaid skort (a skirt-and-shorts-in-one, so you could bend over without showing your panties) and ribbed wool tights. I made the block-long journey to Norquay Annex head down in order to avoid stepping on orange berries that had dropped from the trees lining the boulevard, hating to have their squashed pulp spoil my new shoes.

Our kindergarten teacher, Miss Fedoruk, arranged us cross-legged in a circle on the floor, like she would every day. We poked each other with our elbows and shifted our bums to assert our spot, our place in the classroom, the world, the universe, and I stiffened my arms at my sides like two fence posts.

Then came attendance, and all of a sudden I was small again. As Miss Fedoruk called out names, making a tick on the page at every

"Here" or "Present," the thought of speaking aloud sank me down into myself, as if my head was a cave in which I could hide. When my turn arrived, I had sunk so deep there was no air left to utter the single word needed to establish my presence. My "Here" was a tiny gasp taking great physical effort, as if my voice was a boulder that had to be pushed up from my stomach, past my chest, through my throat and out my uncooperative mouth. I hadn't expected this, I had assumed I would be confident like my big sister now that I was at school, too.

On my first report card, Miss Fedoruk wrote that I was "very soft-spoken and could be encouraged to speak out at home as is being done at school."

"Oy," Mom groaned when she read the note. "What's the matter with you? Why don't you speak up?" She didn't have time for this foolishness, I could see how busy she was, how I was in the way as she fried onions and ground beef for meatloaf or set the table for dinner or cleared it off afterward. She couldn't wait for me to find the connection needed to take the shadowy intimacy of thought out of my head and into the precise consonants and vowels of speech.

ON SATURDAYS WHEN MOM ASKED DAD TO GET US KIDS OUT of her hair, we'd go bowling or ice skating, or, better still, to a double bill downtown at the Orpheum theatre. After settling us in our seats, Dad would head off, returning between movies to check how we were doing: I'd spot my father in the aisle, towering like a beacon above the hordes of children running to buy popcorn or candy. He was allowed to come and go as he pleased without needing a ticket like everyone else, as if the usual rules didn't apply to him, as if he was special.

Dad was like that, his own man, doing things his way. He could snap his toes like most people snap their fingers. He'd toss peanuts one by one into his mouth, then pass the bowl around, instructing us kids to chew them one at a time like he did, as if that was the smart way, the way to really savour them. When Mom asked him to peel apples for her pies, he'd aim to do each one in a single stroke, triumphantly dangling the curving length of red skin in the air when he succeeded.

Other chores he was less keen on, like washing exterior window-panes, which he would tackle only after Mom had asked "time and time again," crying, "Andy, please, I can't stand to look outside any-more!" He'd say there was a quarter going for whoever helped; while Dad climbed the ladder to reach the first floor, my sister and I would do the basement, our hands turning black from the newspaper used to polish the glass. The lawn was his domain, too: he'd offer a penny for every two weeds we dug up, which Mom said was spoiling us.

Dad knew poetry by heart. My autograph book was filled with variations on *Roses are red, violets are blue* (*You and Dennis K. stick together like glue,* or, *God made me beautiful, what happened to you?*), but Dad wrote: *I wandered lonely as a cloud / That floats on high o'er vales & hills / When all at once I saw a crowd / A host of golden daffodils,* signed *Compliments of Willie Wordsworth, Love, Daddy.* His zigzag script was full of peaks and troughs like tracings of the heart's activity on a doctor's monitor.

Mom's contribution, written with a light touch that flowed quickly across the page, made me feel like a movie star: *Of all the fans who've written in this book of yours, I hope you consider me 'The Tops.' Love, Mother.*

MOST SUNDAYS, MOM TOOK MY SISTER AND ME TO BEA-consfield United Church, while the boys stayed home or went to hockey or baseball practice with Dad. My Sunday school teacher, Mrs. Duff, was a large woman with soft, droopy eyes, as if she'd cried too much, which might well have been the case given she was a widow, with as much life behind her as I had ahead of me. I knew this, I knew we were on opposite ends of existence. She was heavy-footed, slow and often still, while I was light and not just fast, but eager, my body popping like corn on one of the child's-size chairs that formed a semi-circle in front of her in the church basement. Mrs. Duff knew things we didn't. Things we needed to know. All adults did.

"If you children want to get to Heaven," she'd say, perched solidly on her much bigger, higher chair, leaning in toward us, "if you want to be with God after you die, you have to be good." She showed us a picture of God, whose hair was snowy white, but whose body, in a pale blue robe, was slender and straight-backed. A girl sat on one knee, a boy on the other, with a handful of children grouped round, everyone neat and tidy in their good clothes. They all had white skin and rosy cheeks, including God. No one looked like the Clarendon Street kids I hung out with: the Irish, whose pale skin was mottled with freckles, sunburnt pink in summer, and the wiry dark-eyed Italians. My family's Russian and Finnish heritage was more indeterminate, my own skin permanently tanned nut brown, while my little brother was a pale blond angel. Nor were any of our bodies as neatly proportioned as the kids' in the pictures: we went through stages of astonishing thinness or plumpness, spending years suffering through a gangly growth spurt or desperate for one to happen. And though we started most days clean and tidy, by lunchtime we had scuffed shoes and tangled hair, dirt under our fingernails, a bandaged knee or scraped shin, tangible signs of our engagement with the world.

Yet I believed in Mrs. Duff's pictures just as I did in my own. Like the house I often drew, with a curly strand of smoke wafting from the chimney and, in the front yard, a tree filled with red apples. Although I didn't know a place like this, with a winding footpath leading to the front door, everything seemed real as I put it down on paper, using crayons and, later, pencil crayons, because I drew this scene for years, always with too many apples, unable to resist adding one more and then one more bright spot of red. Drawing this house and yard felt good, not shifty and foreboding like when you told a lie, but strong and clear, like truth.

Mrs. Duff convinced me that Heaven was a real place in the sky, beyond the clouds, past where the universe ended. Hell was a hot dungeon in the centre of the earth where the Devil and the sinners lived. Heaven and Hell, up and down, good and bad: I sucked it all in, reassured by the orderly Christian universe.

As a reward for perfect attendance, Mrs. Duff gave me a gold chain strung with a small tube containing salt. The necklace came with a piece of paper the size of a fortune cookie insert that said: "Ye are the salt of the earth, Matthew 5:13." My Sunday school teacher was easy to please compared to God, who was the source of so many rules and punishments, and she lived nearby instead of far away in the sky. Her house was on a corner down the street; I'd see her through the kitchen window, sitting at the table with a cup of coffee.

ON DAYS AT HOME, AS LONG AS IT WASN'T RAINING, MOM would send us outside to play, with instructions not to bother her until lunch or dinner. In summer, I might lie on the front lawn and look for four-leaf clovers, their good luck tucked away in the soft grass that, according to Mom, was full of weeds and needed mowing, as if a lawn with short tidy grass was superior to one in which four-leaf clovers and buttercups flourished.

If a friend passed by, we might rub the buttercups under our chins to see if we liked butter, revealed by the amount of pollen left behind. A ladybug might alight on one of our arms, and we'd chant, *Ladybird, ladybird, fly away home.* My friend and I, our voices, the delicate spotted insect: everything was one great swirling mass of energy. Like a van Gogh painting, the world was alive with texture and colour, our bodies throbbing with molecular action. The boundary between us and the air and the grass and the ladybug's tiny tickling feet was porous, so that we were part of them and they were part of us in a world without end.

Sometimes a neighbourhood gang would gather in our front yard. We'd climb the stairs on the narrow edge outside the safety of the handrail to the first step, then jump onto the grass, and then again to the second step and the third, all the way to the top, where I'd freeze.

A boy would be sure to say *hurry up* or call out *chicken*, his words the nudge that pushed me off the edge. Then the worst was over. I knew how to fall, arms and legs loose in their sockets, bones melting into the ground. Our shrieks would eventually bring Mom out, who would chase us away for making such a racket.

We'd head to Ricky and Little Steve's house two doors down. Their property was several feet higher than the one next to it on the north, the drop marked with a low metal rail that acted not as a barrier but an opportunity: something to jump over or off and onto the neighbourhood's softest greenest lawn, made of thick squares of turf, nothing like the weedy lawns our dads grew from seed.

"Let's pretend…" someone must have said, the beginning of an idea striking them as they tumbled onto the grass, a sensation so delightful they wanted more, and they wanted not only to tumble again and again, but to make each fall bigger and brighter, framed with consequence. "Let's pretend…" someone said, and we got caught up in the magic, concocting a game in which a Killer shoots a Victim, who then — here was the brilliance of our imagining — had the perfect opportunity to fall onto that luxurious lawn.

The opening cue came when we spotted a car approaching in the distance up Clarendon Street; the Victim would hurry to the rail, the others forming a group nearby. When the car was almost upon us, the Victim climbed onto the rail, balancing precariously; the Killer stretched an arm out straight in front, taking aim. We'd hold our positions until the car was passing — go too early or too late and there'd be no audience — at which point the Killer pulled the trigger and the Victim exploded into a spectacular dying leap, collapsing happily on the cushion of grass.

I can't recall how the shooting was done. Did we point two fingers and shout *pow*? Or did we use one of the boys' silver cap guns, loaded with a strip of firecracker paper? Either way, it was madly exciting, especially being the Victim, coming up with the most convoluted death throes possible in the too-short expanse of time between leaping and landing — that brief mid-air suspension when everything had to happen, the whole tragedy of dying from a bullet to the heart at such a young age told in an instant to the passing motorist. I'd imagine him reeling from shock, how he might lose control of the wheel and crash into the cement fence in front of the brown stucco house where the road came to a sudden end. (I always pictured a man at the wheel, at a time when many of our mothers didn't drive and "he" and "him" were the default pronouns.) Cars did crash there, speeding late at night, but never during our game. I was always hopeful the driver would call the police to report the murder once he got home, disappointed no one ever showed up to investigate.

Our raucous finale, with free-for-all jumps off the rail, inevitably attracted the attention of the young couple whose grass we were trampling. The couple, who didn't have any children (Why not? we wondered), would yell at us to stay off their lawn.

The boys would troop across the road to play in Mike and Pat's basement, where girls were never invited. That would leave Glenda and me, and sometimes Carmelita; our older sisters had other things to do than join our games. "They think they're so big, don't they?" we'd say hotly to each other. We might wander over to Mr. and Mrs. Low's grocery on Kingsway, looking for discarded pop bottles to cash in for the pennies needed to buy candy cigarettes. On the way back, when anyone passed, we'd hold one of the thin white sticks between two fingers, waving it casually about like our parents did with real cigarettes. The sweet tips slowly melted in our mouths, coating our teeth with a delicious sugary wash.

The Bluebird Variation

MY PARENTS DIDN'T BOTHER MUCH ABOUT WHETHER OR not we kids brushed our teeth, figuring the baby set would fall out anyway. If a tooth started to ache and was a little loose, Dad would tie a string to it and tug. When more complicated measures were called for, Mom took us on a bus ride down 41st Avenue to the older, upscale Kerrisdale neighbourhood where Dr. Springbett had his practice.

In the waiting room, trying to ignore the drill whining across the hall, I'd study the black and white photographs hanging on the walls. They showed our dentist's daughter in short stiff tutus and in long flowing ones, sometimes on her toes, sometimes with a leg extended into the air, the lines and curves of her body expressing a symphony of energetic forces. Mom told me her stage name was Lynn Seymour, and that she danced with the Royal Ballet in London. I know now she is considered one of her era's great dramatic ballerinas, and was muse to a major English choreographer, Kenneth MacMillan. Mom and I didn't care about him, the person who made up the steps. Our attention was on the ballerina, the one who became the dance.

Mom's attention was also on Mrs. Springbett, the well-dressed mother of a ballerina and wife of a dentist, who was occasionally featured in photographs in the newspaper's society pages. Our dad was a truck driver, coming home dusty at the end of each long day, and my parents never went to society events or appeared in the paper. They never went to the ballet together, either, though Mom was drawn to those fancy dancing bodies.

BALLET HAS CLOSE CONNECTIONS TO RUSSIA, WHERE MY mother was born. Its roots are in Renaissance Italy and the technique was formalized in seventeenth-century France, but in nineteenth-century Saint Petersburg the art form reached a height of classical splendour in three iconic ballets set to Tchaikovsky: *Swan Lake*, *The Nutcracker* and *The Sleeping Beauty*. In the early twentieth century, two of the most legendary dancers ever came out of Russia: Anna Pavlova and Vaslav Nijinsky. And one more in the mid-twentieth century — from our time, my mother's and mine — Rudolf Nureyev, who made headlines around the world shortly after we moved to Clarendon Street. Nureyev defected to the West in 1961 while on tour with the Kirov Ballet, running from the KGB agents sent to escort him back to the Soviet Union. "I want to be free," he told French police at Le Bourget airport. Mom and her family had escaped from Soviet Russia, too, though theirs was a private drama that took place decades earlier. Nureyev's was big news contained in the charismatic body of a twenty-three-year-old dancer.

Nureyev, with his mop of brown hair and pouty lips, looked like a member of one of the new boy bands, maybe the Beatles. Or the edgy, soon-to-be-formed Rolling Stones; even standing still, his taut, muscular body looked ready to pounce, to do something dangerous. Nureyev was so popular that before long he appeared on TV, on *The Ed Sullivan Show*, which our family watched most Sunday nights. He partnered English ballerina Margot Fonteyn in an excerpt from *Swan Lake*, his hair shellacked into a tidy helmet.

Fonteyn was in her mid-forties, a few years older than my mom, dancing a romantic pas de deux with this wild child, her composure in dramatic contrast to his broad, reckless strokes. Yet, accompanied by Tchaikovsky, they existed together harmoniously within the carefully composed arc of their movement.

I wouldn't have noticed the difference in age, which was often re-marked on in the press; he was said to have rejuvenated her career. They were both old to me then, like all adults. Mom must have noticed. What would she have seen in the closeness between this mature woman and young man? Nureyev wore white tights and a short doublet that showcased his hard-working legs and buttocks and drew attention to his pelvis — a smooth neutral expanse thanks to his dance belt, so you could, for the most part, ignore the genitals dis-guised and protected by the cup. You could, if you tried, see Nureyev only in his role of Prince Siegfried, a ballet prince who would never subject a woman to the hard thrusting lines and insistent, unmusical rhythms of everyday life and love.

Whatever we noticed in that televised pas de deux, something about the arrangement of artistically expressed physical forces and mute intimate interaction called ballet appealed to us. We weren't the only ones: during that live broadcast, tights and tutus and Pyotr Ilyich Tchaikovsky transfixed many women and girls, and many men and boys, too, in homes across North America. Ballet was becoming a cultural force in the world once more, as it already was in our house: my sister and I had started ballet lessons the year before Nureyev's front-page leap to freedom, when I had just turned six.

EACH TIME MY TEACHER STOPPED BESIDE ME AT THE BARRE, enveloped in a cloud of perfume, I'd breathe deeply as her soft hands gently moulded my body into place. It felt good to be held within the shapes of ballet, entering a wordless space where I was faster and more responsive than my usual self. At home, I inhabited a parenthetical place in the middle of an outgoing older sister who was already good at reading and arithmetic, and younger brothers who didn't have to be yet. If an adult paused to ask a question, my response would take too long to come and their attention would pass, my voice mysteriously disappearing when most needed. At ballet, in my own spot next to the barre, arms and legs, fingers and toes, took me directly into action.

For our first concert, Mom laboured over her old Singer sewing machine making my Bluebird costume. Everything was blue: the tulle skirt, the satin underpants and bodice, the gauze wings edged in sequins, the ruffled hat and the ribbon to tie it under my chin.

In a photo taken on the day of the show, my sister and I pose in front of our house. Angie sprawls gracefully on the ground in her Flower tutu, while I stand in front, slightly to the side. Because I'm smaller, I always stand in front for pictures, and Mom hasn't taken into consideration that my sister is sitting or noticed my tutu fluffs out so much it blocks a bit of her head. You can tell I don't have much technique — I'd been training with Marge Berri for less than a year, and my arms are raised in a wonky circle above my head, one leg lifted, the pointed foot placed smack dab on my kneecap.

My brothers stand on the front stairs in the background, probably thinking they were out of camera range, dressed in their best: white shirts tucked into trousers, a tie on Davie, a bowtie on Stevie. Since Mom didn't drive, Dad must have been around to take us to the theatre — actually, Britannia high school auditorium — and presumably stayed to watch, but I can't recall his presence or, for that matter, his absence.

Onstage, I poured myself into my Bluebird dance, believing utterly in the steps devised by our teacher for a ballet called *Pom Pom*. It took place in a palace garden, for which there was no set, just an oasis of light surrounded by darkness, but the lit space, the idea of a garden, was enough. Inside the choreography, supported by the music, I knew exactly where to go, and when and how, like I didn't in the wide-open expanse of daily life.

Everything went perfectly until the end, when the head Bluebird — the tallest girl — forgot where to exit; instead of leading us off, she ran toward the wings on one side of the stage and then on the other, while we trailed behind. When the music ended, she froze mid-stage. From my spot at the very back of the line, I could see the others stumble to a halt. I did, too, as if our dance had hit a brick wall.

Without the pause it would have taken to find my voice and speak, I turned round. The whole flock turned, too, and as I tiptoed off stage right they followed close behind to the sound of thunderous applause. Well, that's how it sounded to my ears, as if all the mothers and fathers, all the sisters and brothers and aunts and uncles and cousins in the audience were on our side.

"You saved the day," Mom said when she came backstage.

It was the first time I had ever done such a thing.

WHEN I SCOURED MAGAZINES AND NEWSPAPERS FOR PICtures to add to my Mickey Mouse Club scrapbook, in addition to photos of the British queen and her corgis, or women with long shiny hair selling shampoo, I looked for dancers. Using a homemade glue of flour and water, I pasted in photos of a French ballerina in toe shoes, three "Lively Lovelies" in fishnet stockings for a Queen of Hearts fundraiser and a barefoot woman in a grass skirt doing the hula. And a man, in black leotard and tights, standing on a bent leg — a plié — with his other leg lifted waist-high to the front and also bent. One of his hands rested on his raised bare foot, casually, like it was no big deal standing like that.

The caption identifies him as American modern dancer Merce Cunningham, in town for the University of British Columbia's Festival of Contemporary Arts. It wasn't who he was that attracted my seven-year-old eyes, but the splendid shapes in which he held his arms and legs. This grown man, who was about my dad's age, presented himself to the camera the way I had for my Bluebird photo, believing that, without speaking a word, something important was being expressed.

The River Inside Our House

BEFORE I WAS OLD ENOUGH TO DECIPHER THE TIDY ROWS of black markings on the pages of books for myself, Mom read Louisa May Alcott's *Little Women* aloud to my sister and me. Over a few pages at bedtime, she found the joy and sorrow in each scene, bringing to life Marmee, who we all loved, and her girls, Jo, Beth, Amy, Meg. She read it like an actress would, trying to express the dramatic truth within each line, releasing the details of story that lay hidden in the flat printed shapes of the alphabet, parading each character's innermost thoughts with energy and interest.

In real life, with no author to help, individual truths are not so accessible, and my mother found it hard to read actual hearts or get inside actual minds. Real people, with their messy real lives, got on her nerves. For my mother, life was not full of opportunities for companionship, it was a minefield of human obstacles that kept her from the peace and quiet she craved. A minor inconvenience, like me asking for something to eat when it was only a little while till dinner, or my sister talking on the phone, stretching the cord from the kitchen where it was tethered, down the hall and into the bathroom, whispering behind the door, could be the last straw. Or my brothers and their friends might be in the basement playing table hockey or darts when she was trying to nap in order to recover her strength, the boys making such a racket she couldn't stand it anymore and screamed at everyone to go home. "Your mom's at it again," a friend said once as we stood outside my house, and I was ashamed at how much you could hear from the street.

It would be a relief to find Mom resting in bed when I returned home from school; if she was up, maybe in the kitchen ironing, I was bound to do something that aggravated what seemed to be raw exposed nerve endings running just below the surface of her skin. If I brought a friend over, our demands for Kool-Aid or cookies, our taking so long to drink or eat, and our chatter — "Why do you have so much to say?" she'd ask — would make her face pinch and she'd cry that we were in the way, she had housework to do. Our voices were such a hindrance to her ability to carry on. However hard I tried to shrink myself down, my mere presence could be such a burden.

One day I walked through the back door with Jo-Ann, the new girl who sat across from me in our grade three classroom. Mom's nerves instantly raged: I could tell by the way she began crashing around the kitchen. Later, she asked why I would make friends with a "hunch-back" and a "midget," blunt descriptions commonly used in the sixties, often spoken in the same tone as my mother's, the way you might say liar or thief.

My mother was unable to appreciate the unique dynamics of real bodies, with some God-like perfection providing a hard measure against which to judge others. However hard I tried to ignore her harsh assessments, they ate into my perceptions like hungry worms. After all, Mom was my major fount of information and skill-building in very necessary practical terms, and I had no awareness of her own particular human limitations. When she told me a child's physical disability was God's punishment for the sins of their forebears, how could I put this in any context? Such as Mom's habitual, naive defer-ence to authority, including the Orthodox Church she was only slowly leaving behind.

Jo-Ann's cheerfulness made things worse. Instead of following the expected script, where physical difference was tragic, she didn't seem to dwell on hers, daring to be not just forthright, but assertive. My disappointing shyness was more irritating than ever in comparison to Jo-Ann's confidence, so unwarranted in my mother's eyes.

Usually we played at Jo-Ann's, a large wood-framed house built at the end of the nineteenth century and pretty much left to age. The shingled exterior was faded, with peeling paint, and the front stairs and porch had gaps where the wood was rotting in the wet west coast climate. Inside, the rooms were dark and musty.

Jo-Ann's mother had the same friendly personality as her daughter, the same short stature and curved spine. Unlike my mother, she was never resting in bed. Nor did I ever seem to be in her way, not even when my fingertips, greedy to explore the world through touch and texture, left smudges on the polished surface of the dining room sideboard and on the glass of a silver picture frame displayed on top. The frame held a photo of a tall straight-backed man: Jo-Ann's father, who was dead. His parents lived with them, their backs long like their son's, but rounded, heads bowed as if in perpetual mourning.

A rickety flight of stairs led to the basement, where steel bars had been erected against one wall so Jo-Ann could do exercises for her spine. Her mom let me do them with her, keeping watch while we hung upside down from the top rung. It was better climbing here than on the monkey bars at Norquay Park, which tended to be packed with kids who might carelessly knock you down onto the hard pavement below.

DESPITE THE WAY PEOPLE EXHAUSTED HER, MOM LOVED the promise of a special occasion. A clearly defined social gathering, separated from the mundane everyday, filled her with hope. Dad wouldn't cooperate over having fancy adult parties at our place, so Mom had to content herself with occasional evenings out put on by one of her sisters or by Lafarge Cement, with the truck drivers Dad worked with and their wives. And with birthday parties for her kids.

Mine took place in June, the month of roses and pearls. They featured deliriously exciting games of Pin the Tail on the Donkey and Musical

Chairs, and cakes baked from Duncan Hines or Betty Crocker mixes. Occasionally, Mom made cakes from scratch, but the measuring and mixing exhausted her, so I preferred the others. I needed Mom to be in good shape for the party. No matter what, though, by the time she served the cake, her usual fretting was bound to have escalated into anxiety: the butter icing would be too soft, dripping down the sides, and maybe the candles weren't sitting straight. If a few were reused from previous parties, she'd worry they might not last through the ritual of singing "Happy Birthday" and making the birthday girl wish, urging me to hurry and blow out the candles.

In the weeks leading to my ninth birthday, Mom devoted hours to sewing my new party dress. She pinned the Simplicity pattern onto the green chiffon spread across our dining room table, slicing through the delicate material with large scissors, basting the pieces together with long loose stitches. Hunched behind the sewing machine, she connected seams and attached ruffles, the needle pounding in and out, the motor revving up to full speed as she gained confidence or became impatient. When some minor disaster brought things to an abrupt standstill, she'd moan, "This darn machine." The dress did up at the back with four glass buttons shaped like flowers, requiring four finicky buttonholes Mom groaned over.

During the final fitting, I tried not to fidget as she yanked pins kept handy between tightly closed lips. Every time she mumbled something — "Stand still" or "Oy, this hem is crooked" — I froze, picturing a pin falling into her mouth and down her throat, its silver tip grazing the moist pink tissue, and then imagining the blood, the tears. When Mom said to turn round, I didn't move, and she sighed in irritation, thrusting a pin through the gossamer fabric with such force it pricked my skin. She adjusted the sash until it lay smooth against my waist, tying it at the back in a bow.

The dressmaking took a toll: I could tell by the way Mom's face darkened and her movements became harsh and abrupt. The only way to keep her nerves from flaring was to be a good girl, good and pretty and quiet in this beautiful new dress she was going to such trouble to create. Even when it was time to address the party invitations and she announced, "There's no room for Jo-Ann," squashing any objections by saying there weren't enough settings for the table.

My friendship with Jo-Ann had become more complicated after Mom caught us playing in the backyard, Jo-Ann with her doll stuffed under her skirt, moaning on the ground as she gave birth, me in the act of shoving mine up my skirt so I could have a baby, too. "What are you doing, rolling on the ground, screaming like demons?" Mom had yelled. "Lifting your skirts!" She called Jo-Ann a bad girl for playing such a bad game, and brought me inside.

"Why do you play with a girl like that?" Mom demanded, and now it wasn't just Jo-Ann's back that was the problem, but also the fact she knew where babies came from. Jo-Ann was "precocious," one of the worst traits a girl could have. It seemed in that humiliating moment as if Mom had been right about my friend all along. Was this why, when Jo-Ann was excluded from the party, I didn't stand up for her? Or was it the crush of so much bad behaviour — Jo-Ann's, but also, confusingly, Mom's and my own?

At the birthday lunch, I sat at the head of the dining room table in my party dress, hair puffy in front where the curlers hadn't fallen out during the night. Mom was pouring Kool-Aid into glasses decorated with gypsy dancers when the front doorbell rang. I could see Jo-Ann through the picture window in the living room, just the top of her head, which was covered in perfectly formed sausage ringlets: she had also worn curlers the previous night, and hers must have been even harder and more tightly wound.

Mom marched to the door. "You weren't invited," she said, as if Jo-Ann was an annoying Fuller Brush salesman. "The party's already started. What kind of girl are you, to just show up?" She shut the door abruptly. "The nerve of her mother, standing at the foot of the stairs."

It was like turning the page in a fairy tale and arriving at the scary part, where dark forces are unleashed. The rest of the party is a blank, though I am quite sure none of us girls said anything; we were not warriors, too steeped in *Sleeping Beauty* and *Cinderella* to spring to action. My instinct would not have been to save the day as I had in the pretend world onstage, but to carry on as usual. The most important thing would have been to keep Mom's tears from filling the river that was forming once more at my feet, to keep it from raging through the house in front of my friends. What had happened to Jo-Ann was bad, but things could get worse.

By mid-summer, Jo-Ann and her family had moved away. I was relieved: our friendship was ruined and the blame had to be mine. Another family moved into their house, with a girl who was also the same age as me. A new friend, a new set of memories. I forgot about Jo-Ann. That's how it was with everyone who left the neighbourhood: they disappeared completely, the world beyond a vast inaccessible void.

I didn't really believe in the absolute necessity of a strong straight body — it was obvious Jo-Ann, her mother and I shared important feelings between us — but I was already drawn to the extreme stretch and strength of a ballet body. A formal aesthetics of line and shape, embodied by people abstracted into beings called dancers, would come to provide an absolute where the adult me could experience what I learned to identify, guilt-free, as physical beauty.

DAD WOULDN'T HAVE BEEN THERE FOR THE BIRTHDAY party, with its inevitable fuss, though Mom doubtless complained later to him about what she called Jo-Ann's and her mother's brash behaviour. "Zina," Dad might have intoned, the two syllables of her name carrying the weight of his despair. He used to chat with Jo-Ann's mother on the street; in grade twelve, when I ran into her at a bus stop, she spoke warmly and asked after him.

I'd often see Dad outside chatting to a neighbour, taking a break from mowing the lawn or raking leaves. "What's he doing?" Mom would say, banging around in the kitchen. "Why doesn't he get to work?" If he was chatting to Mrs. Cowie, a young mother who lived in the pink house with a white picket fence across the street, she'd shout from the back porch: "Andy, are you going to stand there all day?"

She'd have scoffed at an accusation of jealousy, but everyone was her competitor. Even me; if I talked to Dad for too long, she'd complain about the racket.

~

PREPARING FOR AN OCCASIONAL EVENING OUT, MY PARENTS would take turns rushing out their bedroom and up the hallway, lit for the occasion, to the bathroom. Dad would go first; he'd shave and put Brylcreem in his hair before shaping a thick wave above the forehead. Mom would take longer, adjusting the bathroom mirror's moveable wings to view the back and sides of her head. On one particular evening, which must have been around Christmas, she sprayed a festive silver streak in her bouffant hairdo and screwed on sparkly rhinestone earrings.

When Dad called us into the kitchen to say good-bye, he told us to lock the door and to phone the Dredges, who lived next door, in an emergency. "Come on, Andy," Mom said anxiously. "We're going to be late." They clattered down the back stairs and into the Parisienne, driving off into the night.

Even though Dad had said we girls were both in charge, my authority wasn't very convincing. I was already nine, four years older than Stevie, but only a year and a half older than Davie and the same height, which evened out our ranking in the family. Our sister was a tall eleven-year-old used to taking charge. When we ran their bath, Stevie refused to get in until I left, insisting, "Angie's our babysitter, not you."

Retreating to the living room, I searched the TV listings: the best thing about babysitting was getting to stay up past bedtime to watch a late-night movie. I always looked for a musical, hoping for romance to flicker by on our black-and-white television screen in the dancing of Fred Astaire with Ginger Rogers or Judy Garland, or Gene Kelly with Debbie Reynolds or Vera-Ellen. The frank rhythms of tap, the forthright way the feet carried the body in the twists and turns of the dance, drew me in. Cyd Charisse's muscular high-heeled legs in *Singin' in the Rain* were like thunder and lightning, threatening to knock Gene Kelly senseless. During the really lively numbers, shoulders, hips and pelvis were punched recklessly out into space. In movies, dance could burst forth in a living room, in a nightclub, on the street: anywhere life happened, dance could, too.

When the movie ended, I staggered barely awake to bed. The house felt eerie without our parents, as if it had lost its anchor and was floating in a dangerous universe. I was reluctant to fall asleep, fearing what might happen once I was wrapped up in dreams…

"Sitting on your lap like that! Flirting with you! And you encouraged her!"

My mother's voice, hard and sharp as knuckles, woke me.

"Aww, you're talking nonsense!" Dad said.

"I suppose you enjoyed her making eyes at you!"

Although my parents were back, the house was still floating, tipping dangerously as my mother shouted about how Dad had ignored her all night, how there had been too much talking, too much noise, how she had been left on her own and some woman who went on about politics had got his attention, had got everybody's attention, a woman wearing pants like a man and drinking whisky.

They headed down the hall with a rush of steps to their bedroom, the door slamming shut. I could hear the torrent of Mom's voice but not the words anymore, and brief rumbles from Dad. Her voice got shriller and faster; Dad's, harder and colder. Mom's torrent, on and on … I wanted to go back to sleep, I wanted her to stop, but still she roared. Finally, a heartbeat of silence, followed by Mom shouting, "He hit me! Andy hit me!" It was as if she wanted me to hear, as if she knew I was awake and listening in the dark.

Heavy footsteps hurried up the hall, followed by the sound of retching from the bathroom: they'd been drinking and Dad, who had a delicate stomach, was vomiting into the toilet. When I heard him preparing a bed on the living room couch, the house tipped over into chaos, and I felt sorry for him, angry at my mother for yelling at Dad just like she yelled at me.

In the morning, Mom banged about the house. "I won't stay with you any longer, Andy!" she shouted. She knew I could hear, that we all could as we went grimly about our day.

"You don't care, you don't care about me!" she screamed until her voice was hoarse. Dad didn't utter a word, not even when she threatened divorce. "Haven't you got anything to say?" Mom shouted. "Can't you speak up?" I wanted, too, to hear what he might have to say, because divorce would be the end of my world here on Clarendon Street. And Clarendon Street was the world.

There was only my mother's refrain: "You don't care! You don't care!"

I didn't know how angry I was at my father, too, for not saying anything, for not saying the thing that would reassure Mom because it would also reassure me.

YEAR AFTER YEAR, MY FATHER BOUGHT MY MOTHER CHOC-olates on Valentine's Day, in a heart-shaped box that seemed the height of romanticism, but they were always the kind with soft centres, not too expensive, never the kind she liked. At Christmas and on her birthday, Mom would open his present with guarded excitement — as if fearing the worst, but hoping against hope for the best — then bristle with dissatisfaction. "Oh!" she'd say with a downward drag that made the word ugly and hard. "You got me a sweater last year." Or: "Why a sapphire? And so small." Dad would grin goofily, stoically, stubbornly believing that by not acknowledging the situation, it would be like it never happened. Magical thinking, like my own often was.

My parents' occasional evenings out continued, but if there was fighting when they returned, Dad would make a tactical retreat, preparing his bed on the couch before things got out of hand.

Only those choreographed couples in movie musicals never disappointed. Their dancing always included an intimate duet as they slowed down to weave themselves together, knowing exactly where to go, and when to stop and look into each other's eyes. The women knew the precise moment to fall back and, right on cue, the men were poised to catch them.

I asked Mom for lessons in the movie kind of dancing, but she said tap was vulgar, ballet was enough. She meant classical ballet, with its particular evocation of coupledom that is a hallmark of the form. When we had watched Margot Fonteyn and Rudolf Nureyev on *Ed Sullivan*, the best parts for Mom were probably when Fonteyn was supported by Nureyev, when he stood behind her and attended to her complicated needs for balance and display within the prescribed steps. That was the man, and the woman, of her dreams.

A Small Dance Inside of Me

MOST NIGHTS, PALMS PRESSED TOGETHER IN THE PERFECT isometric action of prayer hands, I still recited the magic words learned at Sunday school: *Now I lay me down to sleep / I pray the Lord my soul to keep / If I should die before I wake / I pray the Lord my soul to take.* Only instead of kneeling by the side of the bed with my sister, I'd rattle the prayer off lying under the covers, pulling them over my head to make a cocoon, alone in my own room now. I'd imagine the darkness inside my head stretching across the universe, taking me to God — but there would be such silence at the other end that I'd toss about in a mess of sheets and blankets, too worried to fall asleep.

Until, switching gears completely, I'd flip into a headstand on the bed, feet against the wall, the head doing the grunt work of support while the feet asserted themselves on top, toes flashing. The restlessness seemed a curse, but the headstand offered comfort: instead of chasing God in my head, I was absorbed by a small dance of muscle and balance.

I hadn't stopped worrying about Heaven and Hell, but next to the salt-of-the-earth necklace in my ballerina jewellery box lay a scarab, a turquoise beetle decorated with hieroglyphics. It came from the gift shop at the Vancouver Art Gallery, representing a whole other set of beliefs.

A friend had invited me to join her family outing to an exhibit of treasures from the tomb of Tutankhamun, the ancient Egyptian boy king. I'd never been in an art gallery, and as we snaked through the darkened rooms in the crush of the crowd, shuffling past the illuminated glass cases, I fell for each artefact in turn — a dagger, an armlet, a bracelet decorated with the Eye of Horus, a scarab with a gold base plate.

The scarab was engraved with a scene showing King Tut standing with a god on either side: Atum and Re-Harakhty, who had human bodies; one had the head of a falcon. All three were the same height and slender build, their heads and legs shown in profile, torsos from the front, an impossible twist that defied logic, their existence in time and space seeming livelier and more complex than ours. Every body in the exhibit carried elegance and power, despite being faded, crumbled or broken, and I forgot the commandment about having no other gods before me.

"Forgot" is not quite the right word because God would always be with me, even when I didn't really believe in him anymore. Back then, though, I mostly did — in the guise of that gentle man in Mrs. Duff's Sunday school pictures, but also in a frightening disembodied form that lurked in the air we breathed, where He could see everything we did, know everything we thought. The business of being good was not easy, and I worried over the many things for which God would hold each of us to account when we died.

Trouble was everywhere, including the weekday walks to and from Norquay Elementary School, which took me past Mrs. Duff's corner lot. I got in the habit of taking a shortcut across her lawn, shaving a few seconds from the journey on the hard cement sidewalk. When she came out one day and yelled at me to stay off the grass, I figured that now I was in grade four, she must not have recognized her former salt-of-the-earth pupil. Mrs. Duff's behaviour came as a shock, though, more evidence of the mutability of all people and all things.

A Warm and Hopeful Place

IN FRONT OF MY FIRST FULL-LENGTH BALLET, THE SHEER presence of powerful, physically engaged bodies sucked me right onstage into every run, jump, toss of the head and lift of the hand. *Coppélia* had been choreographed by Arthur Saint-Léon almost 100 years earlier for the Paris Opera, but it was as if each configuration of individual and group force was being created right then and there. The movement seemed inevitable and convincing, like it had to happen exactly the way it did.

The performers were mostly senior students from local dance schools assembled by the Vancouver Ballet Society; while they might have been rough around the edges, young people — working on instinct, with energy to freely lavish — often inhabit movement most acutely. Among them was sixteen-year-old Reid Anderson (who would go on to direct the National Ballet of Canada and Stuttgart Ballet) in the role of Franz, a village boy who falls in love with a life-size doll he mistakes for a real girl.

In the new millennium, *Coppélia* is not one of the popular classics; it doesn't have the wit of *La Fille Mal Gardée* (in Frederick Ashton's 1960 version of the eighteenth-century ballet, the one I am familiar with) or the beauty of the white scenes in *Swan Lake* and *Giselle*. Also, the passive female beauty at the centre of the story grates as a plot device. In 1965, though, it spoke to something very present in many minds, certainly in mine. Having only recently stopped playing with my Barbie doll, I completely understood Franz's attraction to Coppélia's perfect stillness, the way you could dream into it, the way it could be yours. When I had dressed Barbie up in an evening gown called Silken Flame — a white satin skirt with a red-velvet bodice that showed off her elongated curves and smooth impermeable skin — I had become Barbie, and was under the vague assumption that Barbie, one day, would be me.

That night at the Vancouver Playhouse, Mom and I sat quietly beside each other in the dark as *Coppélia* raced by to the bustling music of Léo Delibes. The seats were filled with women and girls, and some men and boys, all of us dreaming into the dance. Shifting, sighing and clapping in the theatre's warm and hopeful space, our motor neurons sparked and fired so fast it was almost like we were dancing, too. Gorging on every step by every character, melting into the same music at the same time, we were happily lost in the prowess of those athletic, aesthetic bodies, lost but also found in a theatrical event designed to make everyone welcome.

The Chinese Doll

THOSE EARLY DAYS IMMERSED IN SENSATION, WITH THEIR easy blur of the imaginary and real, had been fuelled by an instinctive grasp of how to engage with life from the inside. There was no separation between me and my actions, between me and the world. Then I became aware of the body itself — my body, with its narrow eyes and wide nostrils, the way my thighs spread when I sat down, big bumpy knees, hair on my fingers, how my joints would open so far and no further, how my arms and legs would propel me into dance only as long as I didn't feel too cautious. A slow creep of boundaries had begun, until I was no longer the running and the jumping, no longer the dancing, but the person doing those things; I was no longer the playing, but a person who played.

My friends and I still met up at the park, hanging out on the swings. Only as fifth-graders, instead of exerting ourselves by madly pumping our legs to try and reach the treetops, we kept our feet on the ground, half-heartedly twirling as we talked, usually about boys.

One Saturday, among the gang congregating on the parallel bars was a cute boy who sat three rows over in homeroom class. When he began walking toward us, I was glad we'd been noticed; all of us shy girls were hoping for just that without daring anything that would draw attention except laughing a little louder. He paused nearby, taking aim through his long blond bangs, and fired off one word — *Board!* — in our direction. In my direction: here I was, almost eleven, still with no breasts and no hips, as if I was a boy, not a girl.

I never thought to fire back, none of us did, we took the judgement of boys and men straight to heart, absorbing their role and ours through a barrage of daily prompts. Songs on the radio, like one by Cliff Richards about getting himself "a crying, talking, sleeping, walking, living doll" were in the air we breathed. We bought and traded *Archie* comics in which the shapely figures of Betty and Veronica burst forth in whatever they wore, even to school. *Playboy* magazines lurked on the top shelves of newsstands; I'd found a stash under the couch of a family I babysat for, page after page of naked women with breasts of intimidating proportions. In movies, poured into her dresses, Marilyn Monroe dipped and twisted, tossed and turned herself into a poem about breasts and hips, lips and long fluttering eyelashes.

It's not like I didn't eat — I loved candy, french fries and spaghetti, food that was supposed to be fattening, but it never went to my breasts or hips. After reading about tapeworms, it seemed a distinct possibility one was growing inside my intestines, stealing nourishment. There had to be some reason I was completely failing at being transformed into a woman. When Mom took me shopping for my first bra, we found just one small enough. "When are you going to start filling out?" she asked, and I pushed her from the changing room. The lacy pink bra, size 28AA, was lightly padded, a humiliating ruse, but better than stuffing Kleenex in the cups like another girl had done. The tissue had fallen out in the changing room after gym class, fluttering shamefully to the ground.

A strict gender binary of exaggerated physical proportions was taken for granted and policed by all of us during my youth. We kept close watch on each other, and on ourselves.

OTHER BODY PARTS WERE ALSO POLICED. WALKING HOME alone in the quiet neighbourhood where I grew up, some boys I didn't know approached; as they passed, one fired off another single word in my direction — *Chink!* I took this bullet, too, to heart. He had obviously spotted my small flat eyes and brown skin, the broad tip of my nose and my overbite, like I was a cartoon drawing of a Chinese girl, though I wasn't Asian at all.

My Finnish father had a belly and legs so ghostly white they shocked me when he donned a bathing suit on family vacations. My mother was "pure white Russian" as she often said — proudly, as if it mattered to be pure and white and Russian. I didn't know White was a political term referring to those loyal to the tsar, but I did know it meant Mom wasn't "yellow," like the people crowded into the Kingsway bus on her way home from downtown, who, she complained, talked so loud in their strange language. "Oy," she'd groan, "it gave me a headache." She didn't like me playing with Shelley Lee, even though Shelley, a straight-A student, lived a block away and was the same age. What would my mother say if she knew those boys thought I was Chinese?

My body didn't make sense. I had a perpetual tan I hardly recognized as such: after spending all summer outdoors, my skin would be dark brown at season's end, black at knuckles and knees; when I curled my fingers, the pale skin hidden inside the folds of the knuckles was exposed, the white lines making a striped zebra effect. By the time my tan faded, it would be summer again. Brown skin stood out in 1960s Vancouver, British Columbia, in a city named for an English captain of the British Royal Navy and a province named by Queen Victoria.

Overt taunts were rare, at least toward me, but a quieter racism that took for granted the inferiority of all things Asian was part of how many Canadians thought in the sixties, and that had become part of my consciousness, too. "Asian" meant different, with British culture long established as the standard against which others were judged. The important thing was to inconspicuously pass as some kind of white, which I evidently didn't.

My mother, I suspect, was glad she could go about her day without her Russian roots being obvious. The West's fear of dirty commie spies — those hateful Reds hiding under every bed — was probably a great part of where her insistence on being White had come from. Not that I paid attention to history or politics back when the way things were seemed inevitable, God-given, not human-made. I simply wanted to be one of the ruling class, one of the porcelain-skinned British girls who had to slather on sunscreen at the beach so they wouldn't burn, whose rosy, freckled cheeks, whose open, arched eyelids and tiny nostrils seemed the way bodies should be.

I didn't know how much I looked like my mother, with the same flat eyes, olive-toned skin and dark hair. Our resemblance first became clear to me as an adult, on a visit to Vancouver during a decade living in England. When I walked into my parents' living room carrying my baby, Aunt Rachel, Mom's oldest sister, exclaimed: "I thought you were Zina!" Much later, when Mom was dying, stretched out on her back on the hospital bed with her bare feet poking out from under the sheets, I saw they were like mine, squared off at the top, a good shape for pointe shoes.

As an adolescent, I believed I looked only like me, belonged only to me, and was relieved no friends or family had been there to hear that boy's racist slur, which would have drawn my odd assemblage of parts to their attention. People never asked if I was Finnish or Russian; instead, there were inexplicable questions about China or Mongolia, as if I wasn't the child of my parents. Even if I had looked at a map and seen how close these countries are to each other, it wouldn't have made any difference, not when national borders seemed the natural order and it was taken for granted that nationality defined us at a biological level. Affordable DNA testing had yet to establish the world's deeper shared ancestry in the popular imagination, including my own.

The mirrors and reflective windows I obsessively stared into showed a girl who was an easy target of teeth and nose, skin and bones. This descent into the finite, self-conscious me affected everything.

~

EVEN BEFORE BALLET CLASS STARTED, I SETTLED ON THE
outside as the older girls took over the changing room while they put
on practice clothes, filling their leotards and tights with the authority of breasts and hips. In the studio, they stood confidently when
we lined up in opening position at the barre — heels together, toes
apart, one hand resting lightly on the smooth wood, poised for action.
Warming up, their pliés and tendus were luscious.

Mom had sent me to a new teacher who taught Royal Academy of
Dance technique, and every Saturday morning I bused alone to class
down 41st Avenue, which stretched in a straight line from the city's
east side to the west. I had no clue how the strictly prescribed technique, for which my anatomy seemed completely unsuited, connected
to the spirit of dance. Dutifully, I'd carry on with petits and grands
battements en croix and ronds de jambe à terre en dehors, first one
side, turning round for the other. Our teacher, Miss Gordon, patrolled
the line, a large woman leaning heavily on her cane until it was needed
to prod a droopy elbow or protruding tummy.

When we moved centre floor, I soldiered through port de bras,
chassé passé en avant into attitude à terre and a series of posé en
avant. Assemblé devant and derrière, sissonne ouverte simples in all
directions, pas de bourrée … pretty names and steps, never perfectly
achieved by my bony body. Never perfectly achieved even by the most
well-suited body and temperament, but I didn't know ballet technique
is an ideal that even the greatest dancers chase throughout their careers.

At home, practising on the basement's cold cement floor, I clutched
the back of a chair for a barre. Slogging through the exercises to piano
music from the LP spinning on my portable record player, the structural limitations of my hips were bewildering. Dancing had become
a difficult technical feat, no longer an instinctive expressive release.
Confronted with the intricate demands of style and strength that go

into building professional technique, I seemed to be getting worse at dance, not better.

WHEN MISS GORDON CAST ME AS THE CHINESE DOLL IN *Coppélia* for the annual concert, it was a bull's-eye for the boys who taunted. Before heading to the theatre on the day of the performance, Mom took a photo in our back yard of me and my best friend Wendy, who was the Scottish Doll in a cute plaid kilt. Wendy's light blue eyes gaze out from under a beret set at a jaunty angle on her head, her blond ponytail hanging down her back. I'm stone-faced in an orange-and-turquoise Mandarin-collared jacket, half hidden in the shadow cast by my wide pancake hat, a pudgy-cheeked, brown-skinned adolescent who could very well pass as Asian.

Performing my solo, I was sure the vast reaches of black beyond the stage were filled with people ready to jeer the way those boys on the street had, people who preferred pale white girls in cute Scottish kilts or flouncy dresses like the Spanish Doll's. Turning round on the spot before sitting cross-legged, thrusting my arms out to the front and then to the sides, the index finger of each hand pointed up stiffly like a hateful chopstick. A sad, sleepy fog descended, and I lost track of the counts. This dance was not me, and I never became this dance, pushing through the insistent music only to get to the end.

MY LIMBS HAD BECOME TOO SELF-CONSCIOUS TO CARRY SUCH A lively thing as dancing. When I told Mom I was quitting, she didn't try to dissuade me. And Dad? Ballet was for girls; he wouldn't miss the concerts, if he was ever there — I can't remember, but absence is an elusive state. His and mine: my own disappearance onstage as the Chinese Doll — in cheap and kitschy steps that bore little relation to authentic Chinese dance — had felt safer than being present, but it was a poor strategy in the long term, just another way to avoid being actively engaged in standing up to and one day shaping the realities of the world.

Kisses Like Gifts

BALLET QUICKLY SLIPPED INTO THE PAST, AT A TIME WHEN the future urgently beckoned. Grade six, a baby grade, was also over and done. I wasn't eleven anymore, either, but twelve, which meant almost a teenager, with the tantalizing promise of being one of the big kids at elementary school ahead.

The in-between time of summer break was spent hanging out with Wendy; our rendezvous point, the Canada Dry bottling plant on Kingsway, lay halfway between our homes. Sprawled on the lawn under a cluster of trees at the property's eastern edge, we talked about exercises in *Seventeen* magazine that we hoped would build our busts before grade seven started, the mini-skirts and poor boy sweaters we were saving babysitting money to buy for the fall, who we would most like to meet from the Beatles and Herman's Hermits. We wondered what kissing was like. How did two bodies come so close without bumping, how exactly did two sets of lips line up and connect?

It was my suggestion to practise together. Stretched out on the grass, it was easy to move close and then closer, until our lips touched, and then more than that — the soft tumbling into another person, even through our closed mouths, which was all we knew of how kissing was done. The pleasure was unexpected and, thoughtlessly pursuing the sweetness, I pressed harder. I forgot it was a girl I was kissing or that I was a girl, there was just the kiss.

In an instant, maybe a fraction longer, Wendy pulled away. We'd gone too far, and I admired her for putting a stop to things. I admired pale delicate Wendy for everything.

The following summer, when a boy visiting from Quebec gave me a quick peck on the cheek, I wrote in my diary, "My first kiss!" It's sad not to have credited the other, because it was real, too, something we made happen in those years of waiting: waiting for our bodies to become one womanly desirable whole, waiting for boys to approve, waiting for life to start, not knowing it was already here and now. Not knowing it was already good enough: our bodies and our dancing, and our kisses, too, these small gifts to us from the world, from us to each other.

This Secret Female Space

THERE WAS SUCH A HIERARCHY OF ACCEPTABLE BODY shape and skin colour at high school, as if we were performing our lives for the aesthetic enjoyment of other people. Although that is only how it seems now; then, appearance felt existential, not frivolously "put on" but an expressive and innate manifestation of self-worth. Each time I fell at the bottom of an assessment, the judgement came as a blow and I stepped outside myself a little more.

When our grade eight Home Economics teacher brought in a colour wheel before our final sewing project to help us girls choose material that would flatter our complexions (boys never took Home Ec), it seemed a good idea. I had already bought my pattern for a one-piece jumpsuit that zipped up the front. It was similar to an outfit I'd seen on Twiggy, the matchstick British model whose popularity gave hope to us skinny girls cursed with uncooperative bodies where breasts and hips seemed unlikely to ever appear. My friends were together in the skin group with pink tones, while I was on my own in the green category, a colour I didn't even know skin could be. That I was green like a Martian was the main fact I learned that day, a humiliating one about me.

Keeping that "me" in perspective had become my greatest struggle, the sense of my own strangeness the lens through which everything was experienced. My insignificance as a teenager in a world run by adults clashed with the enormous responsibility, drummed in at Sunday school, of being worthy of Heaven in order to avoid the torments of Hell. Even if I was no longer convinced of the literalness of the Christian afterlife, I worried some kind of final reckoning was in store. More immediately, the intangible concept of an everlasting soul clashed with my finite physical existence in a body that was more present than ever before. My underarms gushed sweat, my facial pores oozed oil and, every month for several days, blood poured out between my legs.

My womb made itself known for the first time in French class; while the teacher droned on about verbs and their mind-numbing tenses, worlds were colliding within. At the break, I stumbled down the hall to the nurse's office, and was sent home. On the lurching journey across Kingsway and up Nanaimo Street, past the Red and White corner store where I bought Popsicles in primary school, the first drops of blood made a wet patch in my crotch.

Mom gave me a sanitary napkin, which I pinned to my panties before falling into bed; later, at the drugstore, I would buy a thin elastic belt to tether the bulky white pads in place. When I woke from a deep sleep, she brought a cup of tea, my reward for coming of age. I would rather have had a public display of breasts and hips, but this womanly going on "down there" was thrilling all the same.

That unnameable region of female anatomy was full of complications and inconveniences. Once my period started early during an overnight trip up Hollyburn mountain with the church youth group, and the leader in charge of the girls only had a box of tampons with her. "Would your mother mind?" she asked. "Have you used one before?" Mom probably would mind, and I hadn't used one before, but there was no choice except to tackle the weirdness of sticking something inside — where exactly? Would it hurt? Would I still be a virgin? After reading the instructions behind the locked door of the toilet cubicle, I took my best guess and plunged in the telescoping cardboard applicator tube.

"You have to touch yourself down there," Mom said when she found out. "You don't want to do that."

I didn't know some women wanted to, or what that might mean. At night, I put a pillow between my legs, rubbing the secret parts against it, overwhelmed by the heat and the insistent tingling that had to be relieved, by the huge pleasure when it was. Afterward, I was baffled and embarrassed by my behaviour.

Boys were supposed to be the ones with bizarre urges, unique to their anatomy, which we girls learned about in Health class. They could be forgiven for relieving themselves alone in their bedrooms due to the extreme demands of male puberty. It got worse when they were older, and our teacher warned us about men who watched dirty movies as they played with their private parts, or who deliberately exposed them to innocent women and girls.

I had already come across the exhibitionist kind of pervert. It was on a Sunday, when the Lord's Day Act prohibiting trade meant Vancouver pretty much shut down and there was never anything to do. My friends and I decided to bus to Stanley Park, where we could visit the zoo and wander forest trails. At a turn near Lost Lagoon, we spotted a man standing under a tree with his pants unzipped doing something fiendish with his penis. Our gang of five turned round and ran off screaming. Later, Glenda's older brother explained what was going on with the "sex maniac's rabbit," as we wrote in code in notes passed, giggling, during science class.

My first experience of male sexuality, the year before, had been more confrontational, yet, on my own, I hadn't dared utter a sound, and told just one friend afterward. The parents of the two boys I was babysitting were planning on returning late, so I was to sleep overnight on the couch. Around three in the morning, I heard them arrive home and go to their bedroom. Minutes later, the father entered the living room, creeping toward me. I shut my eyes, so he would think I was asleep and go away. Only he came nearer, dropping down to sit at the edge of the couch, placing his hands on my chest, his mouth on my face, his breath stinky with booze. My own breath stopped and I couldn't speak, which hardly mattered because my mind had shut down with shame — not so much for me as for this old man of forty or fifty, or maybe he was just thirty, but old in my eyes, married and a father, and behaving this way with a twelve-year-old. With me.

What would happen if his wife heard a commotion and came out? They would fight and it would be my fault. Pretending to be tossing in my sleep, I tried to wiggle out from under the weight of him, out from under his smell. It was the most fight that could be mustered by a good girl who didn't like to make a fuss, who was too polite to argue with someone else's father or with any man in charge. After a few minutes, he staggered off.

I never went back, and never explained why; I wouldn't have known what to say. Aside from warnings to avoid perverts, who were easily spotted and apparently an entirely different order of being, sex came neatly packaged in pop songs and movies, in comics, teen magazines and Sunday school lessons, as romance and love, marriage and a family, leaving me with no idea about what was going on in that man's head. I had such little understanding of physical desire, even my own. My body's longings were secretive and hard to fathom: I couldn't see the new space that had opened inside, and didn't realize the sensations in my clitoris and the yearning in my gut were a call to survival of the species, that my womb wanted to function and find its fulfillment.

At high school, sitting cramped behind a desk, I tried to ignore the ache to be active and engaged. I was a cheerleader one year, but the coveted role required intense jostling for position in our routines and while busing to cheer at the boys' games, calling for social skills that were beyond me. Mostly, I made do watching the fierce physicality in Hollywood musicals, shown in constant reruns on TV. There, lust was abstracted into the formal terms of choreographed duets, in which the same story was told again and again: a story about attraction, excitement, misunderstanding, separation and coming together, finishing with a big bang of bodies like missiles exploding.

~

THE SUMMER BEFORE GRADE TWELVE, OUR FAMILY TOOK what would be the final journey together to visit our Finnish grandparents in Ontario. There were just five of us in Dad's Parisienne; my sister, already at university, was busy with her own plans.

As we crossed the country, passing vistas of uninhabited land on both sides of the highway, the mountains and trees in the distance made powerful statements of colour, shape and texture. I imagined making my way up a mountain peak, easily, as if I were a spot of colour, too, dabbed there in a few swift brush strokes.

We also passed many young men, and occasionally young women, hitchhiking at the side of the road. I envied their freedom, annoyed at the way Mom would click her tongue disapprovingly. She and Dad saw unwashed hippies in torn jeans with knapsacks a hobo might carry, the men with long girlish hair. I saw free spirits.

Crowded together in my paternal grandparents' home, the same two-bedroom bungalow where Dad was raised, the familiar scenarios unfolded: saunas, picnics, my grandparents' bafflement at the drama of their Russian daughter-in-law's reactions to the people and places we visited. They would speak to Dad in streams of anxious Finnish when Mom, perpetually dissatisfied, yelled late at night. The ideals lodged in her mind meant everything real was bound to disappoint, especially when her reactions were boosted by the alcohol the adults were never without at social events. "Zina, Zina, you'll wake the kids," Grandma said once when we were little. "Stop worrying about the kids," Mom had screamed. "It's always about the kids!"

I wasn't a kid anymore: I was a teenager, old enough to go on long walks by myself, hurrying out the door before my escape could be challenged. Putting one foot in front of the other in the straightforward architecture of walking, the inherent optimism of forward motion kept me going, as it still does, full of hope for what might lie around the next corner, or the next one.

On one walk that passed through a neighbourhood park, I met a girl in a long cotton skirt and hand-made leather sandals, with tufts of dark underarm hair and a heavy sprinkling on her legs. It was unusual to see so much rogue hair on a female body, crashing the illusion of innately smooth feminine flesh, separate and distinct from men's. A shock, but impressive.

When some boys offered to share a joint with us, Elaine inhaled with gusto. Not worried about police or troubled by reports of side effects such as brain damage, she lay back on the grass, as unself-conscious and relaxed as a sunbather at the beach. The most I had tried before were Indian cigarettes called Bidis, bought at a hippie store on Fourth Avenue; they looked like joints, and I smoked them with a friend on the way home from school. This was the real thing, which I tried to handle with the same nonchalance as Elaine and the boys.

Elaine lived in foster care, she told me, and was glad there was no one to boss her around, meaning parents. I saw her as a free spirit, like the young people on the highway. Like I wanted to be — and with that thought, an idea shot from my mouth: "It would be great to hitchhike back to Vancouver. If only there was someone to go with."

"Far out!" Elaine said, sounding cool like the three cops on *Mod Squad*, my favourite TV show. "My brother lives there, I've been wanting to visit."

Within a day or two, I arranged to stay overnight at her place, where she seemed to have freedom to come and go, with no foster parents in sight that I can recall. I left a note on my grandparents' kitchen table announcing our plan to hitchhike to Vancouver the next morning, a 2,000-mile journey from Thunder Bay. Later, I would learn Dad had gone out on the Trans-Canada Highway looking for me. What would have happened had he found us standing on the side of the road? Me braless under my yellow tank top, my new friend not used to taking orders from parents and, as I enviously noted, looking ten years older than me, though she was sixteen, a year younger.

That first morning with my thumb stuck out, I didn't have a single thought for family. The world felt free and easy as cars whizzed by while we sang Bob Dylan songs and snacked on dried apricots and sunflower seeds, the kind of food Elaine ate. She had a grapefruit in her bag, peeling it like an orange and eating it wedge by wedge; I had only ever nibbled little pieces from a grapefruit cut in half and doused in sugar, using a spoon to tweak out the pulp.

It seldom took long before a car pulled over onto the gravelled verge. Who needed parents or money or tickets or plans? During each ride, I'd keep a close eye on the driver, especially if it was a two-door car and another man was with him (only men picked us up), leaving Elaine and me to climb into the back with no escape route. I wouldn't have accepted a ride in the truck filled with a group who'd obviously been drinking, but Elaine appeared oblivious to the danger and I followed her lead. She sat in front between two of them, I was wedged in back between two more, watching every move, smiling politely at their banter, silently praying they would release us without trouble. They did, and as we stood in the sunshine waving good-bye, relief rushed over me. Ashamed of my childish fear, I envied Elaine's bravery.

In Calgary, we checked in as usual at a youth hostel, finding an unoccupied bunk bed in a communal room filled with fellow hitchhikers. A young man with ragged brown hair and torn jeans sauntered by — another free spirit, someone with his finger on the pulse of the countercultural times, a saviour of the too-material world. He lived in Calgary and was just hanging out, he said, not as if he didn't have anything better to do but as if hanging out was the whole point of his day, a spiritual practice along the lines of *Be Here Now*, a book by Baba Ram Dass (a.k.a. Richard Alpert) that had just come out. When he invited me to his place — skinny, green-skinned me, not Elaine with her womanly curves — I gratefully accepted.

His one-room apartment was sparsely furnished, with a mattress on the floor. Right away he set about preparing some hash, crumbling it into a ceramic pipe and sucking in the heavy smoke. On my turn, I tried to handle the pipe with the same ease.

Passing it a second time, he said, "I'm glad you're not an uptight chick. People are always putting on a front, pretending to be who they're not. We should just accept each other, be honest and open."

We continued smoking until I was floating, not thinking, ready to prove my honesty and openness by slipping off my top and skirt, feeling grown up and desirable at last. Sex was much warmer and friendlier than expected, a thrillingly intimate experience I hadn't planned on (and almost certainly would have refused except for the hash). But I didn't want it to stop.

Returning to the hostel in the morning to resume the journey with Elaine, I figured I'd proven myself: instead of a middle-class girl who still went on holidays with her parents, I was my own woman. My body's contentment felt like love.

Back home, I told my best friend Trudy how I had met a stranger across a crowded room, and somehow I knew, I knew even then... It took a few weeks to realize the charismatic renegade, whose name has long disappeared from memory, wasn't going to phone as promised. I actually knew nothing. This is when the loss hit home — not of my virginity, with its heavy burden of inexperience and ignorance, but of any confidence that I mattered in the world, I mean automatically mattered, just for the fact of simple existence. I took this man's disposable intimacy as a reflection of my worth.

That year, hitchhiking around the city, each time I was picked up felt like a personal success. Men of every age, personality and socio-economic level would pull to a stop, risking a rear-ender for their sudden decision, cavalierly holding up traffic. Sometimes, after climbing in, I'd see the driver's fly was unzipped; my strategy was to chat as if I hadn't noticed and, when we stopped at a light, flee. I was never sure of a safe exit: often, the passenger door couldn't be unlocked from the interior, so the driver had to get out and release me. Whether or not this was deliberate sabotage I don't know, though it was strange how many locks were like this during my hitchhiking days. With each ride, I accepted danger as the price of being that free-spirited person on the roadside, going where I wanted independent of bus routes and fares.

The red sports car had one of those "broken" locks, leaving me trapped when the well-dressed thirty-something driver took a sudden detour to a deserted street, which happened to be by my old elementary school. There was nowhere to flee when he lunged toward me, pinning me to my seat. It was happening, I was going to be raped. I begged God for help — out loud, though not loudly, my breath deserting me as it always did in a crisis. My pleas were whispered in a fervent religious-person voice, in the wild hope God really did hear and know everything, that He really could make miracles. Appearing more annoyed than angry — as if my not cooperating was merely a nuisance — the man got out, walked to the passenger door and set me free.

I ran past the familiar houses where friends from the elementary school had lived, past the Dragon Inn on the corner at Kingsway, taking the shortcut across my old Sunday school teacher's front lawn to Clarendon Street. It was late and Mrs. Duff's house was dark, but I was running to save my life and wouldn't have cared if she had seen me trespassing.

~

PRAYING FOR GOD'S HELP IN A CRISIS REMAINED A HABIT, though I hadn't gone to church for a couple of years. The impetus to leave was rooted in my body, which led so many of my decisions; this time, it was issues over my voice, put under scrutiny when I joined the Beaconsfield United Church choir. Under the pressure of public singing, a chasm would form in my throat, so suddenly that whatever word was caught spanning the gap broke in half, turning into a witch's cackle. Singled out at practice for not being loud enough, and then for being off-key, I mouthed the words in church the next Sunday, my last with the choir.

Around the same time, my mother, who taught Sunday school at Beaconsfield to the older teenagers, had her class play a Bible study game that involved kissing, presumably as a forfeit during some quiz on church doctrine or history. It seems inconceivable she could have thought of such a thing. While the United Church offered a more relaxed set of beliefs than the Orthodox religion she grew up in, Mom was certainly not physically expressive, not the type who kissed or easily hugged even within her own family. However, the main way Mom related to the opposite sex, a common term of the era she took literally, was to flirt. She scorned women who debated men over politics, or who joined their discussions of baseball or hockey. A flirtatious kissing game — doubtless mere pecks on the cheek — might have struck her as an ideal way to bridge communications between the young men and women in her Sunday school class.

I could hear her talking on the phone afterward to a church official. "You're making a mountain out of a molehill," she was saying, but weakly, losing the battle. An error in judgement was something I could sympathize with, but my humiliation was stronger: I knew the kids in her class from the youth group, and had a crush on one, John-John (the nickname distinguished him from another less popular John).

That was the end of Beaconsfield. Mom's attendance lists, lesson plans and white leather Bible were gone from the dining room table where she would prepare her classes, and the family never returned.

FOR EASTER THAT YEAR, MOM TOOK MY SISTER AND ME TO Holy Trinity, a Russian Orthodox church where, in traditional fashion, there were no chairs or benches. Mom found standing for the lengthy service difficult, so we arrived late in the evening when it was well underway.

At midnight, priests led the congregation outside, each of us carrying a lighted white candle, for a procession that circled the small domed church three times. The burden of being me temporarily lifted in the simple act of walking together in the dark, an act that carried its own optimistic statement about community and spirit. Since the service and songs were in Russian, though, I had only a vague understanding of the actual doctrine we were enacting, about as vague as what I knew about my body's secret bloody desires.

Returning to the Dance Inside

WHEN I HEARD ABOUT A PLACE WHERE YOU COULD LEARN this thing called modern dance, an echo of my former dedication to ballet sounded loud and clear, clanging a big *yes, go for it, this is for you!* At age eighteen, a bona fide grown-up high school graduate, I pursued that echo, which returned the power of corralling time and space through the intense, and intensely transient, expressions of dance.

The studio, called Synergy, was at the downtown corner of Robson and Granville, up a few flights of stairs. I don't recall what I wore that first day, but the standard gear was black leotards and stirrup tights with the toe and heel cut off, designed so bare feet could grip the ground. Instead of a piano, several drums were clustered in a corner, and we didn't start at the barre, though there was one, but at the centre.

"First position," our teacher said quietly, as if dancing was the most natural thing in the world. I put my heels together and turned my toes out, like in ballet; from my place near the back, I saw everybody else had their feet parallel, hip width apart, toes pointing straight ahead, so I pushed my heels out to parallel, too. When we sat down to stretch, I discovered the contraction and release, which seemed key to the meaning of dance. It isn't, I realize now, but the concept is fundamental to the high drama of the Martha Graham technique in which Linda Rubin, our teacher and the studio founder, had trained in New York.

During the contraction, on a long, steady exhalation, the spine curves in and the focus is intimate, personal; in the release, with a slow inhalation, it straightens and lengthens as the body opens up and out. Crashing my way through the precise, demanding floor combinations of Graham modern dance, giddy with breath and adrenalin, every contraction took me deeper into myself, while every release got bigger and bigger, until I felt like a planet or star in a dance of cosmic proportions.

We took turns crossing the floor to finish, launching ourselves from a corner of the room in a series of jetés. Mine were not great — I hadn't danced in years — but the excitement of that mid-air explosion, legs split open like scissors, filled me with hope, or maybe expectation — some sense of energy and optimism. Landing lightly on one foot, I raced eagerly forward into the next jeté and the next and the next. "Go for it!" Linda shouted and I did, abandoning myself to the movement, disappearing into it yet fully myself, and somehow fine with that. At least for as long as the dance lasted.

III

The Mind Is Also a Muscle

ONE OF THE FIRST THINGS I DID AFTER ARRIVING IN Montreal to study at Concordia University was sign up for free student jazz classes. Mostly jazz dance was too earthy and extroverted for me, but I liked the low fast runs and sparkly upward bursts. I took ballet, too, evening classes twice a week at Les Grands Ballets Canadiens. It was good to be standing at the barre in tights and ballet slippers again, sometimes feeling hopelessly inadequate — each time I swung my leg up during battements, my hips would shift depressingly — but other times filled with a huge exciting energy. For a few seconds, a couple of minutes at most, my entire body would pull together, every inch working to fulfill the same goal. "Yes!" my teacher, a redhead with pale Degas limbs, would yell.

At Concordia, I was studying for a degree in Communication Arts, specializing in film, inspired by my discovery of European directors. And of Norman McLaren's *Pas de deux*, made in 1968 for the National Film Board of Canada. Using a stroboscopic special effect, McLaren mapped the arc of the dancers' movement through space, making tangible the in-between moments of their duet, and making something in me tangible, too: a yearning to be eternal and beautiful like the dance and its ethereal tracings. Such were my heady desires and extravagant inspirations. "I want to be a violin note..." I wrote in my journal while listening to Tchaikovsky's *Piano Concerto No. One*.

It didn't occur to me to study dance at university, though York in Toronto had started Canada's first dance degree program in 1970. Even if I had known about it, I wouldn't have been interested. I read about the art form on my own, feeling no need to formalize my knowledge or intellectualize my way in. Not then, not when dancing was so much about expressing myself, and so transformative, turning me into an abstract force through which the universe flowed — the universe or God or spirit, whatever you call the thing that is bigger than a single consciousness and that makes you feel strong and connected, inspired to go on.

With film studies, I discovered another kind of creative encounter that was not about my own physical act of dancing. Interpreting and discussing film drew on everything inside, but in a way that was responsive to the artwork and related to the world in which it was created, and this also made me feel bigger and stronger than my single conscious self. My guide in this new intellectual realm was professor Marc Gervais, SJ.

In Vancouver, I'd had no idea what the initials following his name stood for: Society of Jesus. Father Marc Gervais was a Jesuit priest who looked like one of my favourite directors, François Truffaut. Looking like Truffaut was part of Marc's charm: I was Nouvelle Vague–crazy and Truffaut was among the movement's key auteurs. It's thanks to Marc I knew about the French Nouvelle Vague, or New Wave, and that I used the term *auteur* not just correctly, but lovingly, as a badge of honour for the men whose oeuvre (another new term) we devoured. (A woman, Agnès Varda, was also part of the New Wave; for whatever reason — Marc's interest, the availability of her films — she wasn't a director we studied and I only discovered her later.)

Each week, Marc stood at the front of the lecture hall, chatting easily with the charisma of a movie star from one of the films we were studying. With a lively nod of his head, he would direct the projectionist to run the next clip, shooting his hand into the air when he wanted him (it was always a young man) to freeze a certain image.

With Hitchcock's *Shadow of a Doubt*, Marc pointed out frame by frame exactly how the light and dark fell across the face of the lead character, Uncle Charlie (Joseph Cotten), turning what I had previously considered merely a good thriller into a meditation on evil. With Truffaut's *Les Quatre Cent Coups*, he used the shot of young Antoine Doinel (Jean-Pierre Léaud) looking out from behind the bars of a police van to give a critical homage on the director's humanism. He dazzled us with insights and impressed us with insider knowledge: Marc went to Cannes and knew Ingmar Bergman. Rhapsodizing over the Swedish director's tense relationship with God, he explained how that played out in storylines and — another new phrase — the *mise-en-scène*. "You have to look at the whole *mise-en-scène*," he'd say, training us to pay attention not just to dialogue and plot, but to everything contributing to the cinematic image, including colour: the reds in Jean-Luc Godard's Maoist-themed *La Chinoise* left us breathless.

I DIDN'T EASILY MASTER MARC GERVAIS'S CRITICAL METHOD. In an essay for a course titled L'Époque Classique, I wrote about Jean Renoir's anti-war film, *La Grande Illusion*. "You play the game of immediate interpretation," Marc noted in his feedback, "whereas this should be an in-depth analysis." He eased the blow by playfully adding 007 after his name, like the student identification number beside my own.

Marc called my second essay — a study of D.W. Griffith's silent film *Broken Blossoms* — a "high-class hodgepodge" whose "method is inconclusive and rambled." A glimmer of hope kindled at the final comment: "But you do what you do so beautifully ... it sort of shines."

I had begun that term in The Second Golden Age in Hollywood Comedy (1932–1942), until Marc suggested The Silent Era might be a better fit. My diary from the Hollywood course records what happened. The first entry is distressed over the "chic surface" and "cynical view" on life and love in Ernst Lubitsch's *Trouble in Paradise*. The second entry is on Rouben Mamoulian's *Love Me Tonight*, which

Marc called "a love poem to cinema." I knew what he meant, noting the film's "explosion of cinematic technique": slow motion, fast motion, sound effects like the boom of a cannon when a china vase falls to the floor, a perpetually moving camera. "But how can a love poem be so mocking?" I wrote, despairing over Mamoulian's merry satire on social class. After the "assault on logic" in the Marx Brothers' *Duck Soup*, I switched courses, facing the limitations of youthful high-mindedness.

In true Jesuit fashion, Marc himself was equally at ease with both high and low art. The Sorbonne-trained intellectual in him might criticize the way my essay on Luchino Visconti's *Death in Venice* stayed "inside the diegetical universe" (diegesis refers to the narrative reality constructed by the film), but the tone was softened by the schmaltzy advice: "Get outside of it, blue eyeshz." Get outside the diegetical universe? That was where I lived best: within the constructed world of art and imagination.

WHEN THE ARTIST NEXT DOOR TO THE HOUSE WHERE I rented a room asked me to pose for him, I was happy to give my time and energy to his art. The first thing I noticed about the painting, in which I would be the last of four nudes, was how much skinnier my body was than the other women's. Being thin and small-breasted was fine in ballet class, but didn't a painter need lots of flesh? Sitting naked in the studio surrounded by a comfortable mess of easels, tubes of paint and pots filled with brushes soaking in turpentine, I relaxed, watching him jab and swirl his brush in a palette of colours. As the precise strokes of paint turned me into shapes on canvas, I felt approved of, and really, really visible.

We went a few times to the gallery in Old Montreal where he showed his work and, after the modelling was over, I explored the art scene on my own, becoming a regular at several places on Sherbrooke Street. I carried a notebook crammed in my shoulder bag, ready to jot down inspirational thoughts, but seldom took it out; usually I stood quietly in front of favourite paintings, mostly portraits, hardly moving a muscle. One owner, who must have noticed the return visits, rewarded my dedication by lifting the red velvet rope barring public access to a staircase at the back of the third floor, leading me upstairs to an attic room. The walls were filled with ornately framed, early Canadian oil paintings — Suzor-Coté and Cornelius Krieghoff among them — that he left me alone to contemplate.

I explored live theatre, too, mostly dance, splurging on a lower balcony ticket to see Rudolf Nureyev at Place des Arts, where he appeared in the National Ballet of Canada's *Sleeping Beauty*, partnering Karen Kain. The Russian star was no longer in his prime, as the press often noted, and stumbled badly landing from a jump the night I attended. But I didn't care.

Waiting for the bus the next day, I spotted Nureyev walking toward me on Sherbrooke Street. You couldn't miss him, his big fur coat flapping open so it framed his body as he strutted in tight pants, legs and feet turned out in tall leather boots. I hurried up to him as he approached, my right arm in a sling (I'd broken my elbow slipping on wet leaves), and said I'd seen him last night, that it was a wonderful performance. I spoke fervently, the way fans do, while he stared, head tilted back, lips pursed. Those lips were the only part of his body that looked soft and lazy, too lazy to speak; he just listened and stared.

"It didn't matter that you nearly fell," I blurted, at which Nureyev nodded curtly and strode off, nostrils flaring.

It was a ridiculous encounter, both of us, in our own way, so in love with the exciting moments of his performance. Nureyev blazed a risky physical path that he needed to dance and I, on my part, needed to witness. There was something I had to learn from dance, some knowledge to be discovered.

My only income came from selling roses in downtown bars and restaurants on nights I didn't have classes, so funds for entertainment were tight. I'd fret about missing the bright moments of dance onstage, worrying over how to get my next fix. One day I made an appointment with the general manager at Les Grands Ballets Canadiens to make a pitch for support: I must have told him about being a university student, but have no memory of our conversation. Dance was something I did, and needed to do, but where this would lead was unclear. All I am sure of is my euphoria upon leaving his office with a backstage pass in hand.

That winter, I trekked to Place des Arts through more than one snowstorm in mukluks my parents had sent from the west coast for my first Montreal Christmas. I entered by the stage door; inside the auditorium, waving my pass at the usher, any seat still empty as the lights went down was mine.

Night after night, I gorged on *Carmina Burana*, thrilled each time the male dancer cast as the Roasted Swan made his entrance in the tavern scene writhing on a spit carried high by two other men. I adored *Tam Ti Delam*, set to Gilles Vigneault, who I listened to at home on cassette.

At intermission, I'd study the program, reading the alphabetical list of dancers as if the credits were a poem: Annette av Paul, Jerilyn Dana, Manon Hotte, Sylvie Kinal-Chevalier, David LaHay, Maurice Lemay, Mannie Rowe, Dwight Shelton, Sonia Vartanian … Vincent Warren, the Phoenix rising from the ashes at *The Firebird*'s end.

Over the season, I became more aware of the men who made the dance. (Male choreographers still dominate in ballet, an issue that surfaced widely during the #MeToo movement. Very quickly, the work of a contingent of women choreographers, who obviously just needed opportunities, began appearing on many stages.) *Carmina Burana* was choreographed by someone from Montreal called Fernand Nault. *Tam Ti Delam* was by Brian Macdonald, Les Grands Ballets' artistic director, another Montrealer. I added Nault and Macdonald to my list of great Canadian artists, feeling proud in a way that's hard to imagine post–Pierre Elliott Trudeau.

At the smaller Compagnie de Danse Eddy Toussaint, you could see Toussaint's *Ce soir-là…* set to Jean-Pierre Ferland, another Québécois whose voice I swooned to at home. The company's star, Louis Robitaille, was about the same age as me but impossibly accomplished and apparently fearless in front of so many watchful eyes. His full physical expression seemed an ideal way of existing in the world and made Toussaint's shows important events I had to attend. Back at home, I would compose poems in praise of the dancers and the dance on my portable typewriter.

In one, the male dancer becomes the Prince, while the female narrator, along with the rest of the audience, is the Princess, watching as he creates, waiting to be brought into "his circle of Life." The naivety of those poems is embarrassing, yet there is an enviable blast of enthusiasm, the appetite for life with a capital L evidence of incredible post-performance highs.

"Enthusiasm — 'en theos' — is to be divinely inspired," I wrote in my diary. I also wrote about my self-diagnosis of manic-depressive, which was my way of making sense of the extreme highs and lows, the constant shift between being active and happy, and sad and alone, which was my experience of life. Enthusiasm was an antidote to the "revolting depression" that often descended when there was no dance, no poetry, no film: when there was nothing but me, and nothing but me to write about.

~

IN A PRODUCTION COURSE AT CONCORDIA, MY FELLOW STU-dents, who were mostly men, filmed action-styled narratives; I made a dance film, starring the best dancer in my ballet class. Shot in portable Super8, it began with a collage of quick close-up shots, set to Fred Astaire's "Steppin' Out with My Baby": arms and legs flash across the screen, a foot steps lightly onto the hard pavement, knuckles rap on a door when Astaire sings about knocking on wood. The second half featured Tchaikovsky's *Piano Concerto No. One*, with longer, slower shots as the dancer practises alone in a studio.

The reception from Marc was muted (oh, the critical mind; I get it now), but, on my part, the abstract film was pretty much what I wanted: movement designed to fit the flat screen, not the stage, giving what was then a radically intimate and disconnected view of the body. Shaped into lines and curves of energetic intention, the body said so much, it seemed to say everything.

THE PAY-OFF FOR PERSEVERING WITH MARC GERVAIS WAS to be accepted into Film Ideas. In my last semester, I was one of the chosen — I believe there were twelve altogether — sitting around a boardroom table over which Marc presided, discussing the movie we'd watched earlier in the week. He teased, cajoled and was occasionally impatient — just enough to keep us on our toes, all in the service of his intense desire to know exactly what we thought about a film, a scene or just one frame, and why. Before speaking up, I would have to force myself to get out of my head and into the room, to risk such daring exposure. Despite this barrier of shyness, I was always burning to take my place at the table. Once I showed up after having two wisdom teeth extracted, jaw still frozen, tissue crammed into my mouth to staunch the blood.

We discussed Nicolas Roeg's *The Man Who Fell to Earth* that day, which I'd sat through twice at a downtown movie theatre over the weekend. I needed concrete information for my review detailing the cinematic language used to tell the science fiction story about how America first normalizes and then destroys its visitor from space, played by David Bowie in a low-brimmed hat. Near the end, I quoted the chorus from a Bowie song I had danced to in a crowded nightclub not long before: *There's a starman waiting in the sky / He'd like to come and meet us, but he thinks he'd blow our minds.* Roeg and Bowie were both exploring a world afraid of change, I explained in my review. Marc Gervais wrote that my analysis showed "heroic progress into a new dimension."

What Marc liked about that essay provides a succinct description of how to write relevant criticism: "You really begin to tell us how the art object functions and to integrate this communication within larger cultural observations."

THERE WAS NO INKLING AT CONCORDIA THAT I'D END UP interpreting dance for a living, and it would be a while until I found my way into becoming a critic. My first published work appeared in *New Dance*, "The magazine by, for & about today's dancers": a news item about a dancer friend, a feature about dance on film showcasing *Pas de deux*, and a review of a performance broadcast on BBC. These pieces were very partisan; it was only later, when I was writing in a more sustained fashion for a range of specialist dance magazines and general interest newspapers, and in my books on Canadian dance history, that the bigger picture of an art form with a past and a future would take shape, and dance became about more than my own or any other single personal expression.

Writing turned out to be a good fit. My relationship with the art form could develop without the intense public scrutiny of performing live in front of an audience, or even in front of other dancers in a studio. Making dance, too, is such a public act: a choreographer needs to convince their team that the shadows and fragments they labour over in the studio will eventually come together into something whole. Composing with words took me inside the creative act quietly at home.

I also came to value critical writing for the way it extended the short-lived theatrical existence of most productions by putting dance onto the page, corralling the ephemeral moments of performance into words and sentences that supposedly live forever. I still feel the responsibility of contributing to the public record: the dance itself is gone even before the dancers take their bows, while our writing lingers on.

From the beginning, I wanted my criticism to reflect the kind of close attention Marc taught us to pay film, except I was writing about a live art form where there is no possibility of stopping individual moments for careful study. Not being able to freeze the action onstage in order to check and refine my perceptions took some getting used to. All I could do, then and now, is work hard to stay connected to the

constantly changing flow of arms and legs in time and space, absorbing dramatic textures, snapping photographic memories of fleeting
physical architecture.

~

WRITING ABOUT DANCE IS A FOOL'S JOB, DECLARED ARLENE
Croce, one in which the afterimage — the remembered dance — is
really the subject. (From the preface to her 1977 collection of dance
reviews, *Afterimages*.) The same thing is true in writing about life,
and there are many scenes from the past to which I'd like to rewind,
to study frame by frame in order to figure out exactly what's going
on before committing them to the page. Scenes from childhood, and
also from the Montreal years, such as the day Marc Gervais took me
cross-country skiing in the Quebec countryside.

Afterward, he dropped me off at home in Notre-Dame-de-Grâce.
As we said our good-byes, Marc leaned over and kissed my cheek, an
unexpected move that I accepted graciously, feeling a surge of power
— not in a showy muscular way, but quietly, as if my irresistible female
body was calling the shots at a molecular level. Being present for this
brief intimate connection was an easy thank-you for the wonderful day.

At the time, I didn't dwell on the kiss or on our excursion, and
would have scorned any narrow-minded suggestion of student-teach-
er boundaries being crossed. Decades later, when the kiss began to
play occasionally in my head, the memory was a fond one.

Only now, as I write this in 2019, a different subtext has crept into
the way the kiss resonates. Revelations about sexual misconduct and
abuse from some of the top men in dance, theatre and film have forced
a public conversation around interpersonal politics. What's become
obvious in this zeitgeist is the huge imbalance of forces behind the
movement of my older professor toward me and behind my stillness
in front of him. His force came from the power of a mature man
trained for action, in a position of authority, no doubt complicated

by tensions from an imposed vow of priestly celibacy. Mine lay in the ripe unconscious beauty of a young woman, trained to be polite and responsive, and also to believe in the passion that womanly bodies ought to arouse in red-blooded men.

My male movie buddy when we were at Concordia together once complained that female students had an unfair advantage in getting Marc's attention. I had shrugged off his criticism. If the typical seventies-era scenario, in which women were seen as equal but prettier, brought any perks — such as the ski trip — I was going to take them, relieved my ugly duckling years were over. Men had their own advantage in being entitled to just exist, taking up space thoughtlessly in classes where their sheer numbers made an intimidating statement. As did the fact all our professors were male. We studied men directors, and would have specified "woman director" had a rare example come up in discussion, like we did woman doctor and woman lawyer. We unthinkingly used "he" as the universal pronoun in writing and conversation. No wonder male students were more comfortable speaking up to argue their point of view and be, simply, present.

The kiss could be cut, so it doesn't complicate a chapter intended in part as an homage to Marc Gervais, the King of Film Ideas. He gave me practical and imaginative tools with which to approach criticism, along with a conviction that ideas mattered as much as emotion: Marc loved film, but never mindlessly. He also disdained hagiography. When we were too gushing in our comments about favourite directors, he'd warn, "You're not writing hagiography, you're not writing the lives of saints." If we were talking about a film, he would be the first to interpret the scene in the car for all its elements of light and dark, situating the action within its own time, informed by contemporary currents.

I TURN OFF THE NAGGING HINDSIGHT AND RUN THE KISS once more in my head, letting it unfold in the uncluttered present tense, in stark black and white, like early Bergman. The car's dark interior, where we sit in our bulky winter coats, contrasts with the bright snowbound streets outside. Large snowflakes drop soundlessly, covering the windows. Marc leans toward me, his lips graze my cheek. His movements are supple and light, the way they are in class when he's rhapsodizing about a film or a favourite Hollywood star, maybe channelling the dashing, mischievous Cary Grant.

Who am I?

"You don't put yourself in the picture," my therapist had said when we were discussing my compulsive empathy. "You try to see everything from other people's points of view."

It's what I've done again, shifting into Marc's character, putting him at the centre of the scene.

"I need to know how other people think," I'd explained to Dr. B.

"Imagine how they think," he said.

Yes, of course, I can't really know.

Who am I?

I am Anna Karina, one of Godard's leading ladies, on whom he lavished long intimate close-ups, showcasing her luminous eyes, soft lips and dark bouncy hair.

I am Liv Ullmann, a Bergman star, a pale Swede with cool photogenic despair.

I am all the gorgeous women on screen who I have admired and loved.

I am, then and sometimes even now, sitting quietly, waiting to be discovered, waiting to be found.

My Fred Astaire

BACK HOME IN VANCOUVER AFTER FIVE YEARS IN MONTREAL, reality butted up against the way I remembered things. My parents were smaller, less imposing. They didn't know everything anymore, which I had suspected for a long time, but now for sure I knew things they didn't: they had never taken film studies or posed nude for an artist.

My sister had moved into her own apartment, but my brothers were still at home. When they weren't at university, they hung out downstairs in their bedroom with their LP record collection and a big fish tank that glowed in the dark. I hunkered in my old room, applying pink polish to my toenails or writing in my notebook, feeling closed in by the two rose and two brown walls that I'd painted myself ages ago. Cranking open the window to perch on the sill, I could see across the road to the back of the house where Joey, my boyfriend from kindergarten, used to live. His yard was fenced off from the lane where my girlfriends and I saw a ghost the night we camped out in a tent for my fourteenth birthday. Everything looked familiar and yet nothing was the same, but I couldn't have said why this made me feel so restless.

Dad still left early for work. Mom was a secretary now, rushing up and down the hallway getting ready each morning. She had started taking ballet, a popular form of exercise during the seventies dance boom but a surprisingly physical move for my mother, who had never learned to swim or skate, and had never even swatted a badminton racket with us when we were kids. In a rare wave of enthusiasm, she raved about the ballet classes and about her teacher, suggesting I go with her one day. "It'll be my treat," she said.

Pacific Ballet Theatre School was at the drab mid-city intersection of West Broadway and Cambie streets, on the third floor of a dingy office building. Typical of many studios, there was a worn floor, faded paint on the walls and a well-used piano in the corner. I positioned myself at the barre in front of my mother, who was dressed in a heavy black leotard and tights, the small pouch of her belly comfortably protruding. At fifty-something, she was probably the oldest student in the class, but everyone else was at least late thirties, early forties, and they all looked mature to me. When we turned round to do the opening pliés and tendus on the other side, I watched my mother move in a beginner's tentative, self-conscious way, her feet soft and round in ballet slippers.

I wore a backless pink leotard, fine without a bra even during jumps: my sleek young body was contoured to cut through space, to be active and energetic. Extending a leg to the side, I hated the weak inner thigh muscles that kept me from lifting it higher, holding it steadier, but then we did arabesques and I felt the strong arc of my back and the firm clear point of the foot stretched out behind me.

"That was fun," I said afterward, buzzing with adrenalin.

"Oh, well, I don't think I did my best tonight," my mother worried. "It was kind of nerve-wracking having you there."

GIVEN MY RECENT UNIVERSITY DEGREE, MY PARENTS didn't think much of my usherette job at the civic theatres (we helped people find their seats; the male ushers took tickets at the entrance), but it meant I could watch shows for free. Including dance, when I could pay attention yet again to choreographed bodies that broke the usual rules and boundaries of embodiment and relationship.

Weekday mornings, I bused to the West Broadway studio run by Paula Ross, Vancouver's poet of modern dance. Paula's poetry depended on the strength and structure of the body, and over a summer intensive we were whipped into shape. Our teacher, Donald McLeod, was a member of her company despite crooked legs that gave him a feisty devil-may-care look when he extended one into the air. To build stamina, he had us run on the spot like in gym class and scrabble across the room in crab walks, a variation on push-ups. He showed us Jesus sits: perched on his bottom, legs and arms held aloft in front of him, his knee and elbow joints were bent so his feet pointed neatly down while his hands were cupped like a supplicant's. Grounded and yet uplifted, a Jesus sit was a posture of prayer.

At the end of each class we lined up at a corner of the studio before crossing the floor in twos or threes. Tossing and turning our arms, legs and entire bodies, we navigated a complex path through time and space. When physical memory kicked in and everything unfolded as planned, the choreography opened a maze of fleeting nooks and crannies, and I was flushed with the success of having done the exact right thing at the exact right time.

Occasionally Paula herself taught, shouting at us to work harder, move faster. Her heckling pushed me to be stronger, exactly as she wanted. It was what I wanted, too. Being stronger in dance class seemed the most important thing in the world because of my belief in the body, whose energetic clamour could be harnessed in choreographic terms that brought order and made aesthetic sense. Despite being sweaty and tired, one member of a small band struggling together in an ordinary street-level studio at the distant edge of a commercial thoroughfare, far from the centre of anything, moments of beauty and truth were within reach if I could only get the steps right.

THAT SAME SUMMER, I FOUND MY WAY TO CABLE TEN, ONE of the TV stations that had sprung up across Canada providing community access to the public airwaves. In the new Marshall McLuhan universe, the boob tube could be co-opted as an electronic medium of artistic potential, an idea with which I had fallen in love after reading *Understanding Media* at university.

In my paperback edition, turquoise ink underlines favourite bits. Such as McLuhan's explanation that the millions of dots of light making up the TV image shine through, not onto, the screen, demanding viewers close the spaces in a "convulsive sensuous participation that is profoundly kinetic…" And his declaration that the viewer "unconsciously reconfigures the dots into an abstract work of art on the pattern of a Seurat…" These concepts had fired me up until I could feel the light shining through the screen and onto my skin, generating a vivid sense of possibility that shaped itself into a mission: to put art onto the televisions that were in everyone's home.

Through Cable Ten, I created my first videodance, *Rosalie*. I used a song by Brian Eno to drive the choreography, with no thought about the legalities of copyright. Eno was not a real person, he was a disembodied voice whose music penetrated social spaces worldwide and got inside our heads whether we wanted it to or not. I had a cassette recording of his album, *Another Green World*, which brought him into my home as well.

"Everything Merges with the Night," the song the videodance was set to, came from that album. The dying falls concluding each line, the mournful verses about waiting, night and forgetting, slotted into my brain as if I was made for this music: it spoke to me directly, provoking an instinctual muscular response. The song flowed with the same sorrow of the river that still ran through the house on Clarendon Street, if with less turbulence now, and deep in the music, just like deep in the river, was a young woman. Submerged in every line of the song lies Rosalie, to whom the singer calls, repeating her name like an invocation. The visceral excitement of evoking the music and Rosalie, the river and me, fuelled the monumental task of creating this four-minute piece of low-tech art.

An usher at the theatre who was an experimental filmmaker offered to do the filming. We worked the lighting together, changing gels throughout the shoot so the colour of the studio backdrop was also in flux. When he was at the camera, I couldn't see his face, only the lens in front of him — and that's where I directed my movement, shaping it for the small rectangular screen of the typical TV set in which it would eventually be framed.

Ever since then, watching close-ups of dancers and actors on TV and film, I sometimes imagine the camera lens they are actually looking at, and yet this barely lessens the dramatic impact: like many of us, I am hard-wired as much for make-believe as for the real world.

Later, in the editing suite twirling knobs and punching buttons, I assembled a collage of mid-shots featuring tumbles to the floor and closer shots of an arm or a hand, everything shifting, restless, isolated. By repeating images, time ran in a disjointed loop, reflecting the repetition of the words and the confusion I heard in the melodic line and almost always felt in myself. Over hours of stopping and starting the dance, running it backward and forward again and again, I veered between despair and joy as the movement didn't cut together and then suddenly it did. I'd go home wired, reeling from so much presence in this multi-level technological universe: there I was in the dance invisibly captured on the brown band of videotape, as well as highly visible on the screen; and live, too, in the editing suite, experiencing McLuhan's "convulsive sensuous participation" in my own electronic image.

ART MATTERED SO MUCH — NOT JUST MINE, BUT EVERY-thing out there. At the theatre, the other usherettes usually let me take posts inside the auditorium, leaving them free to chat in the foyer. Over a season, an array of dance, theatre, music and opera was presented; with dance, I'd happily watch the same show more than once from different positions, gorging on the intimate details visible from a close view in the orchestra section, then, up in the gods, appreciating the more formal elements of shape and structure. On evenings off, I might attend a movie or poetry reading, or visit the art gallery on pay-what-you-can night.

Once I took a bus up Burnaby Mountain to Simon Fraser University for a screening of student films. At the end, while the audience shuffled out, a young man ambled over to where I sat jotting down a few last impressions in my notebook and mumbled a question about what I thought of the work. My reply was likely opinionated, either for or against — that's how I tended to experience art then, as good or bad, black or white; either I was all in or all out. When I headed to the bus stop, he fell into step beside me.

John worked with video, too, as many young people did in those days, and I liked having that in common. He liked the fact I was a dancer (men usually did, often assuming this was code for stripper). During our journey into town, we arranged to go dancing, agreeing on a mid-week evening when the nightclub wouldn't be too crowded.

He showed up for our date in his wire-framed glasses and thin-soled high-topped runners. I was dressed for action in ballerina-style flats and tight green pants, hair pulled back in a ponytail. A repetitive disco beat was blasting as we entered the club, so I asked the DJ for something less predictable, thrilled when he put on a gritty song by Patti Smith and then a propulsive one by Bruce Springsteen.

John, as it turned out, was my Fred Astaire. Despite no formal training, he knew how to be present in the dance we made up on the spot, our consciousness pulsing through every molecule in every organ and muscle, in every inch of flesh and bone. We paid attention to each other, without losing our own inspiration, taking turns leading and following in a free unselfconscious flow. Nowhere else, in no other sphere of action, was I able to be both fully myself and yet also so responsive to another person.

Every time we went to a club, our dancing took me into heady fantasies involving the trinity of my body, his body and the music. John would swing me round in cosmic configurations, the music our safety net. We might stumble to the floor, it didn't matter, we'd keep on dancing, punks in tight pants exploding with energy. Existing moment by moment in the dance and in relation to each other, our hyper-conscious movement would trace wider and wider trajectories over more and more space, the sea of people moving back to form a circle around us. My limbs melted into liquid honey, eaten up by all those watching eyes. Especially by John's.

At the end of that first night out, he walked me to the bus stop, waiting patiently for a rare after-midnight bus to arrive, following closely behind as I climbed on board. Neither of us said more than a few words during the journey across the bridge to the North Vancouver cottage where I was house-sitting, or when he passed like my shadow through the front door. In bed, when he was inside me, I wanted to stay connected forever.

The house-sit ended and, back on Clarendon Street, I hated lying alone in my childhood bed, my body heat scorching the sheets. John didn't have his own place, either — he slept on a mattress on the floor in an artists' collective — so I gathered my meagre financial resources and moved into a basement apartment in an old house near the West End beaches. It was paradise jogging along the seawall in my first pair of the thick-soled bouncy runners people had begun wearing, which acted like catapults with each step, and a thrill strolling up trendy Robson Street to go dancing downtown. And to have my own door to open whenever John knocked, a sound that made my skin tingle, my vagina contract.

On nights he didn't sleep over, I wrote poems about the great rocking cradle of sex. Or about watching my boyfriend eat a strawberry tart. *So much concentration / and licking and nibbling / Ooh, it makes me hot.* I had no desire to get pregnant, but my body was its own eager ambassador for my empty womb. Even in public, in the middle of the Mozart Tea Room.

AT A PARTY WAITING FOR JOHN TO ARRIVE, I DID MY BEST to mingle, feeling like a conspicuous outsider who had to prove her right to be present. It was always like that at social events. I'd almost given up expecting him, itching to escape out the door, when there he was, surrounded by his gang.

John made a beeline over, grabbed my hand and led me to a room where people were slow dancing. For a few seconds, I relaxed into the familiarity of being together within the music, before being jolted by an uncharacteristically overt direction as he pulled my arm down, guiding my hand to his crotch. I felt something squishy. He said it was a hunk of meat (it must have been wrapped in plastic, I've forgotten the details) worn for a performance art piece he'd been in earlier that evening.

My recoil was unintentional, but revealing. I was a dancer, whose expression was embodied and whole-hearted. I wasn't interested in presenting an arty theory about masculinity, I wanted to dance a song about John and me against the world.

He started coming by less regularly, busy with his high-concept artist friends, those men and women in black, bodies static and slouched, eyes hooded, unfriendly smoke drifting from their cigarettes. They inhabited a cooler world than my physically enthusiastic one. After a long absence I eventually realized was permanent, I heard he was seeing an older video artist with good art world connections.

I was devastated at how easily John had given up our dance — and dumped me, though I couldn't bear to think of it in such direct personal terms. Recently, we had choreographed our first work together, for a studio event at Simon Fraser University: just as our creative collaboration was growing, he was moving on to something and someone else.

Many nights, alone with my Smith Corona portable typewriter, I banged out desperate poems. *You're like Muzak to me / I think of you constantly / If only you were a symphony.* I read some of them at an open mic session at the Literary Storefront in Gastown, a welcoming place filled with the sincerity of poets. Another evening, very late, I went out with friends and spray-painted my disillusion on the side of a South Granville office building: *I want to conceive / only through the elbows / babies with three legs.* The graffiti, although anonymous, was a way to make my mark and to be seen and heard — if not by John, then any passerby would do.

SOME MONTHS LATER, ASSEMBLING A SHOWCASE OF MY work at Cable Ten, I discovered John was in the editing suite next door. I half-listened to the soundtrack leaking through the walls, managing to finish at the same time as him. As we walked side by side down several blocks, it felt good to be stepping in synch; we were a similar height and build, and our strides naturally matched. Until John stopped to admire an expensive property along the boulevard, declaring his hope to own such a home, and his ambition re-opened the disconnect between us: to me, they were just big houses to which I had no special attraction.

When my showcase aired on Cable Ten, it would have been a shock for my parents to see their daughter plastered over the television screen in those arty dances. I don't recall telling them about the broadcast, but they could have come across it channel surfing. At a later date, they might have caught the videodance filmed at English Bay: I heard from a friend it was shown sometimes when the station had a few minutes of airtime to fill. Set to a breezy jazz flute, close-ups of the ocean and sand, and of arms, hands and feet, were cut against each other like waves crashing on a beach.

I never saw the later screenings because I had left the country, but the thought of those few minutes of dance being out in the world was reassuring. The public presentations felt like an accomplishment, like the birth of something. Actually, they would mark the end of this chapter of my life; if I had known, I might have made different choices ahead. Not that I even realized choices were being made, or understood how, for every action taken, others get left behind.

My Family Dance

STEPPING ONTO THE FLOOR IN MY 1920S DANCING SLIP-pers, a find in an English village antique shop, the familiar feeling of anticipation pushed me forward and into my husband's arms. As our bodies connected, Keith lifted his spine and stiffened his arms to take a formal partnering position, assuming the character of a fond husband shepherding his wife through the stately path of a waltz. The humorous flourish was his actor's way of entering into the peculiarly intimate public display of social dancing. For the whole long waltz, at a wedding reception for Keith's nephew in Manchester, it was glori-ous to be lost in the movement, lost but also found within the steady rhythmic pulse of time.

There had been no dancing at our own wedding reception, a champagne picnic for four in a field of daisies in the countryside near Bristol. Cows grazed in the neighbouring field, the steeple of St. Mary's Anglican Church where the ceremony took place visible in the distance. Marrying an Englishman enabled me to live and work in Britain, but if practical considerations forced the decision, the com-mitment was real. Despite Keith being much older — more than two decades, if I had stopped to count — neither of us gave any thought to the hard facts of our different stages of life. My own understanding of effort and energy had yet to incorporate the small declines as the body solidifies and spreads, gravity having its way, inertia insinuating itself into tendons and muscles.

England was a place of mecca for a young woman from Vancouver, a city where so many British had immigrated over such a long time that their culture and values seemed to be my Canadian ones. Britain was everywhere when I grew up: in school curricula, in local theatres, in bookstores, record shops and newspapers. Actually being there was both reassuringly familiar yet also excitingly new.

I had started teaching dance almost immediately on arrival, lugging my boombox on double-decker buses all over Bristol, where we first settled. At a dancercise class in Totterdown, I mercilessly pushed a group of older women to step-kick to Blondie's "The Tide Is High," reluctantly accommodating breaks to catch their breath in what were to me disruptive moments of rest.

In Hotwells at Hope Centre, a former chapel next to a neglected graveyard, I offered a course advertised as creative movement for eight-to-eleven-year-olds "who enjoy moving with grace and rhythm, energy and joy." The first time I demonstrated triplets — an easy travelling step whose contrasting dynamics I loved, dipping forward and down deep on the first count, followed by two steps high on the balls of the feet — the girls watched from the sidelines, wriggling impatiently. During improvisations, they would jump on tables stored at the edges of the room, swing around structural poles. At first I'd stop them; it could be dangerous, it wasn't part of the plan. But Jane, with her tangle of long brown hair, would scramble with such conviction onto a tabletop and the others would follow.

Hope Centre was a short walk downhill from the flat Keith and I rented in a converted Victorian row house. My small group of students also lived nearby, and, after class, we'd walk home together, the girls jostling to hold hands with me. One by one, as we passed their houses, they dashed through the front door to their mothers until I was on my own, heading toward my front door.

KEITH LOOKED FOR WORK, BUT NOTHING EQUALLED HIS involvement in Vancouver's movie business. He had been an actor, and then built his way up in the art department to his first contract as production designer. There, though, the adventure abruptly ended in the disgrace of being fired, prompting his retreat home to England.

I had met Keith through a friend when that last film — *The Grey Fox*, about Bill Miner, the "gentleman bandit" who committed Canada's first train robbery — was in pre-production. Once the Mercury Pictures office was set up downtown, Keith hired me as an art department assistant. Soon, with production looming, everyone was on edge finding early twentieth-century props and costumes, finalizing the script, firming up locations, scheduling actors and crew. Keith's solution to the stress was to get out of the office in the middle of the day for a few lunchtime beers.

There was evening drinking, too, which began to start earlier and end later, the first sociable beers with friends followed by solitary ones at his kitchen table. If I stayed late enough, I would witness the kind of storm familiar from childhood, except Keith's litany of woe was not domestic — it was about the emotional toll of performing his one-man show, an adaptation of Gogol's *Diary of a Madman*, and how, despite a rave review in the newspaper, there had been no interest from the theatre in-crowd; it was about missing his potter's wheel and the feel of clay in his hands, because he was a potter, too. His litany was about a floundering friendship with *Grey Fox*'s director, Phil Borsos, and a co-producer: they had loved his renderings of people and places, but he was no longer included in the inner circle. More and more the litany was about the dreariness of uptight Canadians, unable to handle a few pints at lunchtime. A pub lunch was a great British tradition and over there no one would give a damn.

The last theme was a response to rumours that the director and a Toronto co-producer were concerned over his drinking. They took me aside to ask how Keith was doing; although daily lunchtime visits to a beer parlour near the office were undeniable, everything else, I reported, seemed fine.

This wasn't a deliberate lie, but to admit problems meant facing those tirades, which had started to include me, always heading off to do my own thing, to dance; I was selfish and wasn't being supportive; I should stop being a neurotic Canadian and shut up about the drinking. Keith's hysterical outbursts were like my mother's, which as a child I had no choice except to endure and also to forgive — how else to carry on? Not that I recognized the pattern. Those were still the days when I thought I was uniquely me, free of any part of the past I chose to forget. These outbursts had to be endured and forgiven, too, never spoken about to anyone, the silence a familiar part of the pattern.

Inexplicably, Keith courted disaster, taking longer and longer lunch breaks, raging over how he was too much his own man to shrink his behaviour because of some uptight Toronto businessman. When he was fired, his team — including me — carried on, invested in what we were sure was going to be a great Canadian film. We believed in *The Grey Fox*, and no one wanted it to fail. Not even Keith, who reluctantly handed over most of his sketches and notes for his replacement.

The Grey Fox is described in the *Canadian Encyclopedia* as "one of the most highly regarded debut features" in the country's history. It won seven Genie Awards in 1983, including one for production design. Keith received no recognition for his contribution, not an unusual omission in the competitive movie business, but it would become a prominent grief in his litany. I agreed with him on this: it was a betrayal, and is an historical inaccuracy, that his name is nowhere to be found in the list of credits.

Mine is there, just the single name, Kaija.

I WAS CHRISTENED SUSAN ANNE. KAIJA WAS MY SURNAME, though it is also a girl's name in Finland. My jazz teacher in Montreal was the first to call me Kaija, a solution to having three Susans in the class.

"Kaija, more grounded," she'd shout, shifting her weight down into her hips and legs in a solid jazzy way I never quite mastered.

"It's a beautiful name," she said. "You should always use it."

My friends in the jazz class liked the sound of it, too, and so did I. Especially because instead of being just one more Susan, I could be the only Kaija. (A note on pronunciation: The Finnish "j" sounds like the English "y." Back then, I would explain that Kaija sounds like the Jamaican word for marijuana, as in Bob Marley's song, "Kaya," with its refrain: *Got to have kaya now.*)

The universe itself seemed to be sending a sign when I read about the concept of ka — the vital and eternal force within us — while researching ancient Egyptian literature for a media culture course. The "ka" in Kaija turned the name into a talisman I wanted to keep close.

In one of my therapy sessions, I had breezed through the story of the rechristening. Soon after, I told Dr. B, I started teaching a dance class called Body Hieroglyphics, something I considered pretty interesting.

"I'd like to talk more about changing your name," Dr. B had said, a rare interruption. "How did that make you feel?"

His question unleashed psychic forces I hadn't known were there. In one disorienting moment, my temperature plummeted, my bones began rattling and a few strangled words broke through the sudden storm: "Free, it made me feel free."

I grabbed my coat to stop the shivering, while Dr. B carried on as usual. Slouched in his chair, notebook on his lap, his pen glided just a little more swiftly over the page. The world also carried on: through the window, I watched a woman walk onto a high-rise balcony, bent with the effort of lugging a potted evergreen. She plunked it down in front of the railing, a whole tree contained in a pot. You see them like that all over on condo balconies and patios. How do they fare in such restricted spaces, how do they become themselves?

"It's like I wasn't a ghost anymore," I said. "I didn't have to be Susie, I could be me."

Back in Vancouver with my family, I was Susan again. But when I met Keith, he preferred Kaija, too. When we married, I had a new surname. Susie and her troubles seemed all in the past.

OVER ABOUT FIVE YEARS IN BRISTOL, KEITH COULDN'T FIND
any lasting work, so when he received an offer to run a museum video
program in his hometown of Manchester, we moved north. As we
were pretty much broke, I was relieved to get a production job at
Granada TV. Typing camera scripts, logging footage on film shoots
and tracking continuity on *Coronation Street* and other bread-and-
butter television fare wasn't what I felt called to do, but earning an
extravagant union wage as part of a team carried its own excitement
and power.

My husband and I lived very different realities, partly generational,
though I didn't yet realize how cultural and political currents bump
and nudge and occasionally push us into our individual selves; I
thought everyone was self-determined, shaped by our choices toward
and away from people, ideas and events. That shifted the evening
I joined him and his friend Clark at the pub, where Keith downed
pints of beer nightly — rich room-temperature English beer, he often
pointed out, not cold North American piss, making the drinking into
an act of national pride.

Clark, I discovered, was born the same year as me. Although he was
raised in the English industrial town of Scunthorpe, far from my own
childhood by the ocean and mountains of Canada's west coast, we
knew the same music and movies, and had the same understanding of
that complex construction called manners: the way a person exists in
relation to others.

And in relation to time. As we chatted over pints of beer (them)
and house wine (me), it was clear that Clark's and my future stretched
forward further than the past behind us stretched back, but it was the
opposite with Keith. I didn't know what this meant, or that it meant
anything at all; it was just something I became uncomfortably aware
of. Our focus on the journey that had to be taken was constantly
interrupted by the equally strong instinct driving Keith to turn back
to where he had already been, past successes and failures preying on
him equally.

Those two decades between us were not abstractions of time and space: they were a monumental expanse of real experience, contained and processed by the complicated biology of an aging brain. I don't mean the obvious ravages of dementia, just the increased load of memories, coupled with the reduced efficiency that eventually slows down every biological function. Thought is one of them: however elusive, it is not disembodied, but right here, within.

DURING OUR WALTZ AT HIS NEPHEW'S WEDDING, KEITH had led and I had followed, easy enough to do within the embrace of a traditional duet. Later that same evening, our baby was conceived. Dance, love, sex and procreation converged, and my womb was happy at last.

Our daughter was born at dawn, to birdsong. When maternity leave ended, I returned to work, mostly film shoots around Britain and France. The usually welcome adventures were compromised by the ache of missing my baby, but Keith was unemployed again and it was up to him to stay home and babysit.

A river sprung up inside the century-old brick row house in which we lived. On my side was my first child, first job as researcher, first time filling in as director for a few hours; on Keith's side, his third time as parent, credits on VHS copies of old films he'd worked on, the gazebo he built in our tiny backyard, a shadow of one designed years ago for a film set. My behaviour after he was fired from *The Grey Fox*, when I had stayed to see the filming through, gained prominence in his litany of woe: passion for art had trumped my loyalty to personal relationship.

It had become obvious Keith's anger originated in a source deep within that would never run dry, and, as a mother, my instinct for survival was strong. Determined my child would not grow up next to a river's edge, in 1991 I escaped such dangerous terrain, returning with her to Canada.

~

THE DESCENT FROM MARRIED WOMAN TO SINGLE MOTHER was a shock, abruptly landing me in a problem social category. Though I bristled at the sympathy my new status tended to automatically generate, I took advantage of a few hours a week of government-sponsored daycare, needing all available help. Then, and at night while my three-year-old slept, I would set up my Panasonic electronic typewriter in the front room of our one-bedroom apartment and get to work. I was barely paid for those early reviews and essays, which were mostly about dance, and it was hard finding a space for them in the world. But in the hush of our own home, I did my best to be there for my child, and also, through the writing, for the dance.

In later years, during writing workshops I gave at Vancouver's Dance Centre, I would describe this early period of motherhood as a rich and fertile one in which I established myself as a dance writer. I would credit a fortuitous meeting with Lee Windreich, a well-respected dance critic and historian, who was happy to find a fellow enthusiast. Lee was also an editor at *Dance International* magazine, which was run out of a small office in Vancouver's West End. He brought me on board as a reviewer, and soon offered a quarterly column in which to cover the local scene. Going to shows on a regular basis, and writing about them for *Dance International* and any other outlet I could find, became a central part of my life.

My parents were already Grandma and Grandpa to my oldest brother's two kids, looking forward to summer visits when he and his family flew over from Ontario. Now they had their third grandchild close by, and became keen babysitters. The revelation was how closely my mother connected with the demanding needs of a toddler, eager to understand and to satisfy them if at all possible. When she had to retreat to bed for peace and quiet, Grandpa was there to take over, grilling salmon on the hibachi or cooking his specialty of scrambled eggs and chopped wieners. On most days, the river in their Clarendon

Street home was a trickle, having dried up over the years since they were on their own.

It was an odd déjà vu to see my daughter play dress-up in my old bluebird tutu, to see how easily imagination could fuel flight. For a few years, she took ballet classes, first with a childhood teacher of mine: Lorraine Smith, who offered classes at a nearby community centre. Now an elderly woman with heavy theatrical makeup, her long hair dyed a dramatic raven black, Lorraine told me about her former glory as one of Vancouver's first professional ballet dancers, performing at Theatre Under the Stars in Stanley Park.

During a demonstration for parents at the end of a session, the girls had to run on tiptoe around the room, the farthest boundary marked by a chair. When it was my daughter's turn, instead of going around the chair, she ducked down and scooted through the open space underneath. The other parents chuckled, and I was proud of the way she had spontaneously defined her own path.

~

MY THERAPIST TALKED ONCE ABOUT A DEPRESSED PARENT'S inability to show positive emotions and behaviour to their children, to reflect positively back to them. He meant my mom. But at the time of our sessions, I was a parent myself, struggling with my own anxieties. I told Dr. B about a birthday party for my daughter when she was primary school age, how I had collapsed in a huddle in the kitchen, crouched in a corner, hidden from view. The table was set, the decorations were up — and the idea that no one was going to come, that the party would be a disaster, had taken hold. Reeling from my inability to make everything all right as a good mother should, a sense of worthlessness — a feeling as clear and certain as love or hate — kept me on the ground.

It took several minutes to find enough strength to force myself upright, to impersonate the competent adult I wanted to be. The pretense worked well enough to allow life to continue: guests arrived, and a friend who is a children's performer put on a fun warm-hearted show.

Those moments of collapse — and many others like them — were a great part of the motivation that kept me going through the hard slog of therapy. If I didn't want to be a damaged mirror for my daughter, I had to see the process through.

IV

Behind the Wheel

BEFORE TAKING THE BRITISH DRIVING TEST, I SIGNED UP for lessons from a professional, despite having held a Canadian licence for almost a decade. I had lost my nerve on the road. The scratches and dents inflicted as a teenager on my father's Parisienne were bad enough, but then, in my early twenties, I crashed my employer's car.

When I landed a job as film director Paul Almond's personal assistant after graduating from Concordia, he often sent me on errands that meant driving around town. His car had a manual stick shift his wife taught me to use, and which made driving even more stressful, but I tried to suck up the challenge as the price of working for the man who made *Isabel*, *Act of the Heart* and *Journey*, an atmospheric trilogy starring Geneviève Bujold.

One morning, I dropped off camera equipment for repair at a strip mall on the outskirts of Montreal. Waiting to exit the parking lot, a steady stream of traffic blocked access to the highway, my view hampered by a parked van. After what seemed a ridiculously long time, feeling I'd be there forever, I mustered courage: spotting a slightly longer gap in traffic, I put my foot on the gas and hurtled forward, only to find myself spinning round in the middle of the road, having collided with a truck. The accident was deemed no-fault, which I gratefully took as the truck driver's act of generosity; now, though, I suspect he'd been speeding and really was partly to blame.

A week or so later, I had to retrieve Paul's car from the garage, finding it parked in a cramped corner. Turning the steering wheel to keep clear of the cement wall mere inches away on the driver's side, I began reversing out, panicked when the car's rear end angled dangerously close to the wall. I turned the wheel the opposite way, intending to gently swing in the direction of the vehicle parked on the other side and also only inches away, but continued moving toward the wall. The physics of cause and effect had vanished, along with any knowledge acquired during lessons from Dad about longer response time in reverse. I kept changing the steering wheel's direction, swinging this way and that until the sickening sound of metal on cement ended the ordeal.

It was a relief to pass the British driver's test the first time, and I began to brave winding country roads and multi-lane roundabouts with more assurance in the second-hand Alfa Romeo, with stick shift, my husband had bought. Back in Canada, I felt confident about my driving skills. My daughter and I stayed at first with my parents, and one morning as we were leaving to bus to Central Park, Dad suggested lending me his car.

"I'll move it out of the garage for you," he offered.

This was something he had always done; the single-car garage, constructed at a right angle to the driveway, had minimal wiggle room. I said I'd be fine, settled my toddler in her safety seat and buckled myself into Dad's dark brown Toyota Corolla. He came to watch, standing by the rhododendron bush at the edge of the driveway. As I slowly backed out, he whipped his hand round in the air to encourage the necessary sharp turn. Cautiously, I swung the car's back end to the left, the corner of the garage looming in my side-view mirror. "More, more!" Dad shouted. Lifting my head to stare through the rear-view mirror at the forceful circles of his commanding hand, I obediently turned the steering wheel more — and heard a soft thud of metal on wood. I saw Dad wince.

Neither of us knew what had just happened. In my own stew of emotions, there was anger at myself for once more being defeated by the fact of unbending metal and at Dad for his insistent direction, and for directing me at all, as if I was a little girl who couldn't do things on her own. There was disappointment at the way I had so easily abdicated responsibility — and now we didn't know whether or not I could manage this manoeuvre, but for sure neither of us wanted me to try it again. And for sure neither of us could understand why, since Dad was such a good driver, I wasn't.

After his death, whenever I was behind the wheel of Dad's last car — the beige Toyota Corolla I inherited — that wince haunted me, but sweetly. Every time I started the engine, my first teenage trips around the block in the Parisienne were also eerily present. In Dad's spot at the helm, the car had felt massive, swallowing me up in mechanical operations that had nothing to do with my desperately biological relationship to life, fuelled by the demands of a newly mature body.

Once Mom was gone, too, all kinds of memories crowded in, not just of her and Dad but of everything, as if the past was trying to return. At the theatre, watching the Royal Winnipeg Ballet's *Romeo and Juliet*, a host of favourite Juliets and Romeos, and defiant Mercutios, tumbled into mind. Lawrence Adams, my editor, was one of the Mercutios: I've seen snippets on film of his performance with the National Ballet of Canada, where he approaches his character's death with bravado. The same way Lawrence approached his own death from cancer. "Bark if I start rambling," he instructed during a telephone call not long before the end, high on morphine.

The memories became so insistent that life was difficult to process moment by moment, making it a challenge to get through the most ordinary day. This, along with a lifetime's burden of secrets and shame, created the oppressive tangle of time that helped land me in psychotherapy.

At first, sessions with Dr. B created an equally oppressive self-awareness, but eventually, once there was room inside to breathe more freely, I could look beyond myself. It was an enormous relief to be curious, instead, about the past inside my parents. Traces of the little girl within Mom and the boy within Dad must have been embedded as deeply in them as my childhood was in me. Of course, I'd had no notion of this when I was little, when my parents were powerful giants, a mother and father without beginning or end, just like the universe.

Finding Sibelius

MY FATHER IS FINNISH, I ALWAYS SAID, TAKING THE CANA-
dian part of his identity for granted, though it was the opposite with
him: he was proudly Canadian, taking his roots for granted and never
double-barrelling his nationality. "Finnish" explained the other language he spoke, different from my Russian mother's other language.
When I got a pen pal in Helsinki through the *Sun* newspaper's Sun-
Ray Club for kids, Dad taught me some basic words: Suomi; tyttö,
poika; yksi, kaksi, kolme.

Dad had his own music, too, by Sibelius, which he listened to on
the occasional evenings he wasn't downstairs with us watching TV.
I'd hurry into the kitchen for a snack while the ads were on, glimpsing
him in the dim light of the living room. Sibelius, coming from an old
78rpm record, would fill the corner where he sat with a small glass
of whisky.

My own CD collection contained lots of Tchaikovsky and
Stravinsky, Russians closely associated with ballet, but after Dad's
death what wasn't there — any Finnish composers — became glaring-
ly obvious. I bused downtown and bought two discs: *Notes on Light*
by a contemporary Finn, Kaija Saariaho, and one by Sibelius, making
sure *Finlandia*, the title I remembered Dad listening to, was on it.

Back home, I tore off the cellophane wrapping and read the liner
notes, which described *Finlandia* as an eight-minute orchestral piece
composed by Jean Sibelius in 1899 during Finland's long struggle for

emancipation from Russia. Dad was born near the Russian border, in Jääski, in an area called Karelia. Pursuing a more stable political situation, the family immigrated to Ontario in 1924. In 1940, when Karelia was forcibly taken over by Russia, my grandparents must have followed the fate of their homeland closely.

In 1951, when Antti, their youngest son, married into a Russian family, they didn't travel to the wedding, which took place in Alberta, in St. Pokrovsky Orthodox church. During the ceremony, the priest placed crowns on the heads of the bride and groom, a sign they would be king and queen of their own kingdom, the home, to rule as servants of God. My father wouldn't have been able to follow much of the ceremony — he didn't speak Russian — but he looks happy, his hair and moustache carefully styled, in photos of the day.

AFTER PUTTING ON MY NEW CD, I POURED A WHISKY AS *Finlandia*'s buzzing undercurrent began. Nestled on the couch with my glass of Crown Royal, the same brand Dad drank, I heard again the music's swirl of strings, then something brooding and gentle, like a scorch of whisky in the throat. Finally, a fireworks ending — brooding, passion, battle, *Fin-laaaan-di-aaaah!*

RECENTLY, WHEN I FOUND OFFICIAL DOCUMENTATION online for the family's arrival in Canada on the SS *Frederik VIII*, I realized that Antti, my dad, was only six months old at the time. Somehow, growing up in a cold-water bungalow on Marion Street in Port Arthur (which became part of Thunder Bay in 1970), he absorbed the culture and language of his birthplace. Many Finns had settled alongside them, in their house near Boulevard Lake, where Andy (always Antti to his parents) and his brother Mike (Mikko) swam in summer. The family also owned land a few miles out of town, building a sauna and farmhouse there.

On our summer visits, we swam in the same lake, even when it rained, the way Dad had as a kid. Grandma still washed dishes in boiling water poured from the kettle; when I helped with the drying, they were almost too hot to hold. The beaver dam was still at the entrance to the road into the farm. In the long grass that still grew by the farmhouse, where we went for a weekly sauna just like Dad had as a child, Grandpa found a magic grasshopper that laid a quarter, which he pressed into my hand. As in the past, the kids had the first saunas and my grandparents went last, when the heat was scorching. Neither spoke much English, their voices merging with Dad's in the gently percussive melodies of Finnish.

Dad said little about his childhood, not when my own and my sister's and brothers' early years were unfolding so urgently, with the boys on his team like we girls were on our mother's. The boys took violin lessons, like Dad had. "I walked to class through the alleys," he said once, "so my friends wouldn't see me carrying a violin and call me a sissy." I have his class photo: six boys wearing ties, eleven girls in their best dresses. Andy stands in the back row, straight blond hair combed off his forehead, the corners of his open mouth tweaked optimistically upward, a smile ready to break out the moment the formality of picture-taking ends.

At my father's funeral, his best friend, Jorgie, told me about their boyhood schemes to earn spending money. They would fish for pike or strip bark off willow trees to sell to the tanner, who put the bark in vats with water and soaked hides in it. Or the boys would head down to the rail yard, swing themselves into empty grain containers when no one was looking and sweep up bits of wheat to sell as chicken feed.

That's how they funded Saturday matinees. The first 100 kids to arrive at the 1,000-seat Colonial movie theatre paid only a nickel, so they made sure to arrive early. Tom Mix was their favourite star. "Tom Mix was a real cowboy," Jorgie had said. "He worked on a ranch and could really ride."

Jorgie also talked about how he and Dad joined the navy together, signing up as soon as they were old enough. Dad operated the ASDIC, the system used before sonar, on the HMCS *Waskesiu*, finding and tracking U-boats (German submarines); he and a partner were on duty when the *Waskesiu* became the first Canadian frigate to sink a U-boat.

"Your dad was responsible for sinking that sub, and should've got a medal. He never talked about it much, though. You always had to squeeze stuff out of Andy."

The *Waskesiu* rescued four survivors, scooping them from the cold North Atlantic water. At a reunion organized in 1999 by the Canadian veterans, in Prinyer's Cove, Ontario, a dinner was held in honour of the remaining German survivor, who flew to Canada for the occasion. When I asked Dad what it was like meeting their former enemy, he smiled and shook his head. "You can't hold anything against one man," he said, meaning one person, an individual at the mercy of powerful political forces and bound, too, by their own most likely quite ordinary character. Dad didn't explain all that, adding just: "It was good, we had a good dinner."

Like Jorgie said, you had to squeeze stuff out of Dad. But there had always been too much happening in the present, with its urgent forward propulsion, to wonder very much about his life before I came along. Now that Dad is gone, no longer in the present and with no possible future, I am left only with the past. For the first time, I want lineage, craving a story that goes back, filled with Dad and also with my grandparents, Klaara and Antti, and with their parents, too, grounding us together in our Finnish roots.

WHEN THE FINAL TRACK ON MY NEW CD BEGAN — SIBELIUS'S *Violin Concerto in D Minor* — I poured a second whisky. It was getting dark out, so I switched on a table lamp. As the whisky's heat filled my mouth and throat, I thought of Dad sitting in the semi-darkness with the amber liquid slipping down his throat, winding its way through his intestines and resting in his belly, like it rested in mine. The concerto was as mad and moody as anything by Tchaikovsky; for some reason, Sibelius's passion surprised me. I played the track again and again, not wanting the intricacies of the violin to end.

~

IN 2011, BALLET BC ANNOUNCED A MIXED BILL FEATURING
Finnish choreographer Jorma Elo's *1st Flash*, set to the opening and
closing movements of Sibelius's *Violin Concerto in D Minor*, the same
concerto I discovered after Dad's death. The night of the performance,
far from being a critical "blank slate" — an impossible state for any
human being, but still believed in by many — my personal connection
to the music bubbled away inside.

Taking a familiar aisle seat at the Queen Elizabeth Theatre, I was
glad there was someone next to me on only one side: my guest, who
wouldn't mind the rustle of my note-taking (I was reviewing the show
for *Dance International* magazine). Without taking my eyes off the
action, I scrawled a flurry of images, most of which would be almost
undecipherable. It didn't matter: the act of putting the dance into
words on paper helped define and retain impressions in the rush of
live performance.

In my review, I would write that I "fell for" *1st Flash*, for the way
"a low arabesque rests for a full moment in a gush of strings," for the
"spins and leaps that surrender to the violin's dizzy momentum." But it
was at the end — when the whirl of sound and image was at its peak
— that I really fell. I had already made that transformative leap across
the footlights, my motor neurons were already firing, but in those
last moments my father came to mind. All of a sudden, there he was
beside me. We were caught up together in the music and the dance.

Nesting Dolls

EVERY OTHER SUMMER, INSTEAD OF HEADING OUT TO Thunder Bay to visit our Finnish grandparents, we made the shorter journey to Alberta's Peace River district to visit our Russian ones on the farm where Mom grew up. Before setting off, she would hand me a paper bag in case I got carsick, and my siblings and I would squabble over who got to sit beside a back seat window. We'd play I Spy and spot out-of-province licence plates; by suppertime, her nerves would be on edge. "We should stop and eat," she'd say anxiously as we approached a roadside diner.

Dad would ignore the tension in her voice, and just like clockwork — or so it seems in memory, as if this scenario happened on every trip — he'd say, "I want to make it a little further. We have a lot of miles to go." Mom had never learned to drive; he'd get no break at the wheel.

Five or ten minutes later, moans from deep inside my mother would erupt, and soon she'd be crying, "Oy, my stomach, I can't take these hunger pangs."

There wouldn't be a diner in sight as Dad drove silently on. The inevitability of what was coming sank me lower in my seat.

"I told you we should have stopped," Mom would wail. "You never listen, I need some nourishment!"

Dad focused hard ahead while Mom groaned beside him on the highway that seemed to never end. She launched into one of her rages — we called it nagging, something mothers and wives were considered prone to — lamenting her hunger, Dad going his own way, us kids making too much noise, and there was no diner, when would there be another diner? "Jesus jumpin' catfish!" Dad would explode. "Zina, can you be quiet?"

Arriving at the farmhouse the next day, words I couldn't understand would pour out of my mother's mouth: weightier vowels and consonants that had a different rhythm. Russian, she was speaking Russian, and so were my grandparents, my uncles and aunts, all the Russian voices streaming together. The hot flow swirled around as I took stock of the old furniture and plain wood floors of the farmhouse, of the kitchen cupboards enclosed with thin cotton curtains hanging on string. I'd slip away to find the outhouse, following the dirt path to the wooden shack, fastening the door with the spindly wire hook, alone with the bugs and the smelly hole where I perched my bare bottom. At bedtime, I had to climb a ladder through a trapdoor in the ceiling to get to the attic where we kids bunked on the floor in sleeping bags.

At breakfast, Baba, a tiny smiling woman in wire-framed glasses, spread my toast with pale oily farm butter, nothing like the hard yellow margarine we used at home. When she spoke to me, Mom had to translate into English, and repeat my reply in Russian.

Grandpa, a thin old man with a white beard who knew only a little more English, drove us into Hines Creek once for pop. After he parked the truck in town and we crossed the muddy unpaved road, a gang of boys appeared calling him Father Christmas. Jeering, the boys followed us down the sidewalk, which was wooden, not cement like at home in Vancouver. Grandpa didn't say a word, not then, and not when we sat at the counter in the café sucking our sweet fizzy drinks through straws, the ice cream in my Coke float slowly melting. I don't suppose he said anything back at the farm, though I don't know what the adults talked about in Russian.

THROUGHOUT OUR VISIT, MY MOTHER'S PAST WAS RIGHT next to me, but I never noticed: the farmhouse where she grew up was simply about our family vacation, my summer holiday. I didn't wonder if boys made fun of the bearded Russian men when she was a child. I didn't wonder where Mom's bedroom had been or whether or not she'd played in the attic where we slept. Or had that been her bedroom? I didn't wonder about this other language she spoke, an impenetrable rumble that defined my mother in a different way than her English words and phrases, precise, often angry units of sound I could understand but usually didn't want to, and had tuned out from an early age.

Only when I was a bit older, in grade five or six, when Mom would sometimes talk about her distant past, dropping a few crumbs about growing up on the farm, only then did I feel it was safe to half-listen. Those crumbs now form a meagre trail pointing in her direction. I know that Sam, the eldest sibling, skinned the gophers they caught and sold their pelts, and that Rachel, the oldest girl, bought caramel corn to put in their stockings one Christmas. I know they gathered dried manure from the fields for fuel, that they had a long walk across the fields to get to school, that the girls had to put rags in their panties during their periods.

Once, remembering parties, Mom's voice brightened and her face opened. And me, too, I opened up with her as she recalled how the men drank vodka and her uncles danced, crouching on the ground and kicking their legs out in front of them, Russian style.

"Like this?" I shouted, fired up with my mother's excitement, crouching down and kicking my own legs out, a boy's step I'd learned in character classes during ballet lessons.

Mom's mouth stretched in a bumpy line across her face and I thought she was going to smile. Then she got her familiar anxious look, and I knew my dancing was getting on her nerves. I clambered up, suddenly graceless, confused by the way my enthusiasm had abruptly ended our conversation.

OVER THE YEARS, MOM DROPPED A FEW CRUMBS ABOUT MY grandparents, too. One of her sisters claimed Grandma was the daughter of a mayor: "claimed" was Mom's word, as if the information might not be true. Was that in Ufa, where Palegea was born? Mom said Grandpa didn't have as "high a standing" as Grandma — those are her words, too, perhaps awkwardly translated from the Russian in which the story had been told to her; I didn't think to ask where he came from or how his parents earned a living. I've no idea how Palegea and Feodor met. Mom only said: "Dad took Mother for a ride in his troika, and refused to bring her back. She had to marry him."

More than once Mom hinted how fierce Feodor could be. "He took things out on Mother," she'd say. He was "old-fashioned," his beard a sign of his Orthodox faith. She'd brighten to add: "Dad was in the Czar's White Army." The hand-tinted photograph in my parents' bedroom showed a black-bearded man in leather boots and dark slim-fitting uniform, a contrast to my mental image of him in white. The Bolsheviks — the Reds Feodor fought against — didn't believe in God, she said. It wasn't until I was a teenager and watched David Lean's *Dr. Zhivago* that I understood a little about the politics of the Russian Revolution and the ideologies behind the Communist Reds and Czarist Whites.

Mom saw *Dr. Zhivago*, too, when it was shown on television.

"It's a great film!" she raved. "That's what it was like for us!"

When the Russian Revolution began in 1917, Feodor was conscripted into the Czar's army. He and Palegea were living in a Siberian village, Novgorodka, or Little Novgorod, where they had relocated from Western Russia with family on Feodor's side, drawn by the opportunity to own land in an area with good farming soil. In the summer of 1923, with Bolsheviks confiscating land, forbidding religious worship and murdering dissenters, they felt they had no choice but to flee Russia, then called the Union of Soviet Socialist Republics (though never by my mother's family). Feodor and Palegea had four children — Simeon, Raisa, Kapitalina and Natalia — and another was on the way.

Three days before departure, my mother, Zinaida, made her ill-timed entry into the world. This was the event from her past Mom repeated most often; each time, her face stretched out loose and formless as if there was no centre holding it together.

"Mother and Dad thought I wouldn't survive the journey, so they stopped to baptize me."

The baptism was in Blagoveshchensk. From there, they travelled up the Amur River to the heavily patrolled Chinese border, en route to Harbin to join a large population of Russians who had arrived years earlier to work on the Chinese Eastern Railway. These aren't facts Mom told me; I found them in a family history: a sprawling tale of immigration covering 100 years — 1894–1994 — written by her cousin. When I inherited Mom's copy, I searched for each small note about my immediate family, and then, for this memoir, devoured those rare details once more. For my mother, though, the journey out of Russia was about one intimate unrecorded moment hidden in the bottom of a boat crossing into China.

"Mother put her hand over my mouth to muffle my cries."

She'd say this like it was something she could remember herself, and only now she's gone do I realize someone must have told her. Palegea? One of her sisters? Did they use the word "muffle"? Surely it was more than that in a life-and-death situation requiring the newborn baby make absolutely no noise. Her mother's hand must have felt heavy and oppressive, stifling any sound that might come gurgling or wailing out of Baby Zina's tiny mouth, any sound and any breath, too.

IN CHINA, THE FAMILY LIVED IN A ONE-ROOM SHACK, SUS-pended in that cramped space between two massive absences: Russia, which they had abandoned, and Canada, known only for its promise. Feodor left almost right away for Alberta, where he took on work as a harvester and sold badger skins to earn money for the others' steamship tickets. He wasn't present when Zina began to crawl and babble — Russian words, of course. Soon she was toddling, then talking and walking, then playing house with a stick she found and cradled like a doll.

Zina was four when Palegea and the five children made the ocean voyage. During the crossing on the *Empress of China*, somewhere in between Harbin and Vancouver, "Zina climbed the stairs onto the deck and earned a few coins" entertaining passengers with a Russian folk dance. Maybe their siblings were with them, but Aunt Kay (Kapitalina), who told me the story after Mom's death, remembered only Zinaida skipping through her steps.

Soon after arriving in Alberta, Zina's "dark and luxuriant hair" (Mom's description, from the family history) was cut off right down to the scalp because of lice. To ease the indignity, Palegea and Fred (Feodor) bought Zina a bonnet from a catalogue, which she wears in her first photo taken in Canada.

In it, Zina peeks out from behind her hands, the bonnet a heavy burst of white on top of her head. Behind her and her sisters, an empty clothesline runs the length of the porch; a skeleton fence is in front of them, made up of just the top rung nailed to the posts. The slats of the perfectly finished half-open gate are carefully cut to form a graceful arc that suggests there would be finer things to come.

FOR WEEKS BEFORE WE LEFT ON OUR LAST FAMILY VISIT TO Alberta, my mother was on the phone getting updates about Grandma, who was dying. Mom's anxious Russian stream of worry and concern overflowed into our home as she waited and waited for Dad's holidays from Lafarge Cement to start. Once we were on the road, Dad drove almost non-stop, grabbing a few hours of sleep overnight at the side of the highway, all six of us camped out in the Parisienne.

When we finally arrived, the car was engulfed in brown clouds of dust as it bumped over ruts in the dirt road leading to the farm-house; even with the windows shut, the air was suffocating. Pulling into the yard, Dad stopped the car abruptly and everyone rushed out. Startled as always by the tall grass, by dragonflies like tiny helicopters, by dry prairie heat, I crossed the yard and entered the house slowly.

It was dark inside, but I could see Baba slumped in her rocking chair. Mom knelt in front of her, moaning.

"Get the kids out," Dad said.

I already knew the worst had happened. *If I should die before I wake, I pray the Lord my soul to take.* That's what I said every night, on my knees next to my bed, palms pressed together in the hopeful symmetry of prayer hands. It wasn't my grandmother's death that sucked the air out of me, it was my mother's epic moans, upstaging the quiet last breath. In that tableau was a glimpse of Baby Zina, who this time would not be muffled.

This is something I only understand now, as an adult, when the complicated trajectory of time often brings the past into the present, right beside me. Whenever that scene in the farmhouse returns, my mother's cries carry a whole history.

~

JUST BEFORE MOM ENTERED PALLIATIVE CARE AT VANCOU-ver General Hospital, we shared our last meal, at a Russian restaurant. My teenage daughter came with us; we chatted until Mom scowled and said, "You two have a lot to say to each other." So we were quiet, listening to Mom air her complaints, mostly about the waitress' slow service. "Oy, where's the food? I'm starving," she kept saying. This time, she really was: her oesophageal cancer had advanced to the stage where she could hardly get food down her throat. I only understood how bad it was after our meals arrived: Mom chewed tiny morsels, taking each one out when she thought no one was looking to hide it under a napkin, unable to swallow anything.

We ordered perogies and borscht, some of our favourite Russian food. She'd left Russia so young, yet the country had a hold on Mom and, through her, on me. Russia was always the place where good things came from. Like the uncles' Cossack dance, and the red kerchief Mom sewed for me one summer and called a babushka. And the piroshki stuffed with hamburger and onion she'd spend the morning making; they were always a little heavy and greasy, but I liked them all the same. One night she showed me how to cross myself in the Russian Orthodox fashion (up, down, right, left), which seemed superior to the way we did it at Beaconsfield United Church (up, down, left, right).

At Easter, Mom would bake a tall round loaf of kulich with raisins and candied fruit. She'd greet me on Easter morning with "Khristos Voskrese!" ("Christ is risen!"). I was supposed to answer "Voistinu Voskrese!" ("Indeed He is Risen!"), but she had never properly coached me so the ceremony fizzled out, though she'd carry on with the triple kiss.

Baba, babushka, da, nyet, spaseba, dosvedanya: my vocabulary is minimal. But as a child I loved to hear Mom speaking Russian on vacations at the Alberta farmhouse or when relatives visited us in Vancouver. The thick dark tangle of her Russian voice was rich and mysterious, not sweet but somehow enticing, like molasses tossed through the air.

That voice and the raging one, too, are within me still. I've come to picture us like a set of Russian nesting dolls: my mother inside me and her mother inside her, in a series of mothers and daughters going endlessly back and back and back. Going forward as well, with me inside my daughter. Though what that means is not my story, but hers.

V

My Mother, My Dance

WHEN I WAS STARTING OUT AS A DANCE CRITIC, MY MOTHER would occasionally come with me to the ballet as my guest. She would dress up in an elegant, often new, skirt and top, with a gold or pearl necklace and large clip-on earrings, generously applied lipstick and rouge, and powder that caked at the sides of her nose. There would be Kleenex in her pocket and, in her purse, a supply of gum and cough candies.

In the theatre, I would take my customary aisle seat, Mom beside me clutching her program, which rattled every time she shifted. She'd sigh heavily and unwrap candies in an effort to soothe the dry cough that harassed her the moment the lights dimmed. Mom was never particularly moved by the dancing, and sometimes I wasn't sure she was really even watching or, if she was, if she approved. Once, making a queasy face, she commented on the way the men's tights emphasized their cheeks, and I squirmed at her use of cheeks for buttocks, which turned the body topsy-turvy. The literalness of her gaze stripped the movement of its abstraction, destroying the balance between staring at a body and being absorbed by line and shape.

Mom would sip a glass of wine at intermission, disappointed I wouldn't let her buy me one. "I'm working," I'd explain. We'd stand next to each other in the crowded lobby, barely talking, never mentioning the dance. I tended to take copious notes during performances in the early days, concerned to get the details right in my reviews: not just who did precisely what, but when did they do it? What did they wear, what was the lighting like and what was happening with the music at key moments throughout? Mom never expressed curiosity on what all that scribbling in the dark was about.

On the drive home, she would start fretting, usually over how Dad was getting on with babysitting back at my place. Any attempt to interrupt her anxious monologue would only increase its intensity; the torrent had to run its course. Outwardly focused on the driving, if the performance had been a good one I could lose myself in favourite moments. Like the white act of *Swan Lake*. A really good Odette fulfills the formal values of the bird-like choreography with strength and precision, but still invests every move and pose with her own musical response, her own dramatic colour, bringing personality to form.

"You didn't talk about the dance," my therapist said when, years later, I described our visits to the theatre. "What would your mother say about your reviews after they were published?"

"Nothing, I don't think she read them."

Dr. B looked up, his expression typically neutral except for a glint at the back of his eyes.

"My parents didn't subscribe to any of the newspapers or magazines I wrote for," I explained. The glint in Dr. B's eyes softened into what looked disturbingly like sympathy, exposing the chasm between Mom and Dad and me.

Back at my condo, Mom would want to know the practical details of Dad's evening: what he and my daughter had for a snack, when she had fallen asleep. One time Dad changed the topic, quietly commenting that he had seen one of my reviews in the *Globe and Mail*.

"I didn't know you read the *Globe*," I said.

They were giving copies out at the grocery store, he explained. "You wrote about Ballet BC, run by that fellow ..."

Before he had finished, before I had supplied the name of the artistic director, Mom snapped: "Andy, what are you talking about that for? You're not interested in dance."

Her brusqueness had its usual effect: Dad and I fell silent. We thought that if we ignored Mom's harsh words, it would be as if they had never been uttered.

When I related our conversation to Dr. B, however, I felt their full impact, and it was like being slapped in the face. Seeing Dr. B's eyes soften again, being taken for the sort of person who needed sympathy, only made it worse — I did not want to be, or to be seen as, someone who couldn't cope!

"Instead of encouraging your father's interest," he said matter-of-factly, as if reading my mind, as if sympathy was nothing to get excited about, "your mother prevented it."

His observation, with hindsight obvious, was another of his precisely cut keys, only this one was thick and heavy, forcing open a place where there was no more thinking things out, there were only two little girls shouting "Look at me!" I was one of them, the other was my mother. "Look at me!" she was saying, her voice louder and more powerful than my own. We were two children standing close to the river's edge, my father on the other side.

Under Dr. B's patient gaze, another memory — of being a very small girl playing in my parents' bedroom — forms in the space separating my mother and me. I'd sneak in when she was busy in the kitchen or downtown shopping, dressing up with the tangle of shiny necklaces that filled her jewellery box and clumping around in high heels from her closet. The room was an alluring treasure trove, including, on the wall above the dresser, a dove-grey painting of a ballerina in a white Romantic-era tutu, her arms held up to frame her face.

When my siblings and I cleared out my parents' home after they were both gone, we took turns picking things for ourselves; on one of my turns, I chose that painting. I chose it thoughtlessly, instinctively, and once I went to hang it, realized there was no place for such a sentimental portrait of a dancer on my own walls. The ballerina floats on impossibly slender pointe shoes as if ballet were a simple gift of anatomy and grace.

The painting has nothing to do with the constructed, aesthetically potent art form that dance has, over the years, become for me. Now this unwieldy artefact from childhood, with its ornate plaster frame, takes up space in my bedroom closet under my dresses and skirts, a link to the past I can't bring myself to toss out.

Finale

WHEN DAD LAY DYING IN A HOSPITAL BED IN THE PALLIA-
tive care ward, I drove Mom for her first visit. The moment we entered
his room, they looked at each other with sharp frightened faces. As if a
magnet was drawing her to him, my tiny old mother moved straight to
my father's side, where they kissed greedily, noisily, smack on the lips.

It was a moment of shocking erotic proportions. Finally, like the
climax of a Hollywood duet, the kind that comes at the end of a movie
filled with plot twists, bad timing and missed connections, my parents
heard the music and danced. And I was there to see it, to celebrate
the subtext about life and desire, about absolute forgiveness and love,
and to mourn the terrible price of their knowing these things, which
was the closeness of death. There was nothing maudlin about the sure
trajectory of my mother's movement toward my dad, nothing tragic
in the heavy lift of his head a few inches off the pillow to meet her
lips, nothing mournful about the rhythm and shape of Andy and
Zina's duet.

Acknowledgements

"MY MOTHER, MY DANCE" WAS PUBLISHED IN QUEEN'S
Quarterly in Fall 2011. The encounter on the street with Rudolf
Nureyev found in "The Mind Is Also a Muscle" was published as
part of a collection called Stories of Encounter in *Dance International*,
Spring 2016. "Nesting Dolls" was published in *Wherever I Find Myself*,
an anthology edited by Miriam Matejova (Caitlin Press, 2017). All
three were revised for this memoir.

I am grateful to Fran Brafman and Karen Wilson, whose patience
over a rough and long-ago first draft went beyond the call of friendship.
Mary Kelly and Imogen Whyte provided collegial support and welcome hilarity as the three of us got together to form our own creative
non-fiction writing workshops, held in cafés and over dinners at our
homes. Thank you to Jennifer Chan for sharing many conversations
about memoir, my own and others. Thank you to Celeste Snowber for
creative exchanges and project support over coffee at our inspirational
Calabria Sessions.

Charlotte Gill at the Banff Centre in 2013 provided expert guid-
ance on what became "Nesting Dolls," with much appreciated critical
conversations with my fellow Writing with Style participants. Group
writing and movement sessions in Ingrid Rose's Lagoon Studio two
years later helped keep the energy flowing.

Moira Farr offered the first professional edit of an early draft with
much good sense. Several drafts later, and close to the end, Evelyn Lau

offered the second professional edit: her poet's expertise in looking deeply into language, structure and the human spirit were humbling.

Thank you to my therapist, Dr. B, whose belief I could pull off what became *Falling into Flight* helped kick-start the adventure. Thank you to Karen Haughian and her team at Signature Editions for bringing the project to a fine finish.

Deepest appreciation to the entire cast of characters portrayed within these pages, for whom, in some cases, names and identifying details have been changed. A very special thank-you goes to my daughter, Jessie Pepper, for her trust and support, and to my parents, who had, so unfairly, no say in the matter of their starring roles.

All errors and limitations are my own.

About the Author

KAIJA PEPPER HAS WRITTEN THREE BOOKS ON CANADIAN dance: *The Man Next Door Dances: The Art of Peter Bingham* (Finalist for the 2008 City of Vancouver Book Award), *The Dance Teacher: A Biography of Kay Armstrong and Theatrical Dance in Vancouver: 1880s–1920s* (Honourable Mention for the City of Vancouver Book Award). She has contributed to numerous national and international magazines, anthologies, journals and theatre programs, and was co-editor of the anthology *Renegade Bodies: Canadian Dance in the 1970s*. She is a dance critic for *The Globe and Mail* and has been the editor of *Dance International* magazine, now web-based, since 2013. She holds an MA in Liberal Studies from Simon Fraser University.